Rommel: The Life and Battles of Germany's Greatest Field Marshal

Rommel: The Life and Battles of Germany's Greatest Field Marshal

By

John H. Stone

Vij Books

New Delhi (India)

Published by

Vij Books
(*An Imprint of Vij Books India Pvt Ltd*)
(Publishers, Distributors & Importers)
4836/24, 3rd Floor, Ansari Road
Delhi – 110 002
Phone: 91-11-43596460
Mobile: 98110 94883
e-mail: contact@vijpublishing.com
www.vijbooks.in

Copyright © 2024

ISBN: 978-81-19438-79-2 (PB)

Contents

Introduction

The memory of Erwin Rommel, a man of action whose military leadership was both outstanding and controversial in the 20th century, is still being remembered and argued by historians and military enthusiasts. The "Desert Fox", as he was known, was mostly remarkable for his audaciousness and, at the same time, his ways of solving issues that others claimed were not possible, especially in the Battle of North Africa during World War II. Therefore, Rommel's skill as a tactician became his legacy, and it is well preserved in the military history records. His lifetime and career, on the other hand, are much more than his prowess in the fight; they provide a multi-faceted picture of a person who was in conflict both personally and in leadership and how it was to control a command under the Nazi regime.

In fact, Rommel's service in the military dates back further than the outbreak of World War II. Hailing from Heidenheim, Germany, a side of the world he was born in, in the year 1891 he was very much attracted to the tough career of a soldier. His outstanding career during the battle of Caporetto especially brought his name on the side of the officers who are considered to be completely strong. His activities after the wars witnessed him rising above others in the army of the Weimar Republic and as the writer of "Infantry Attacks," a book considered as the foundation of the small-unit tactics that showed his talent as a thinker and a problem-solver. This biography tries to access the stage where these years were his, suggesting how these were building blocks for his future strategies and his view on leadership.

On the eve of World War II, Rommel's creative commander capabilities were coming to the surface more and more. The 7th Panzer Division he was in charge of during the 1940 invasion of France by Germany played the needed strategic advantages in military art that the Germans were to use in this conflict. His genius in this campaign was double: his superiors loved him very much, and his idol Adolf Hitler spotted him, offering him a command in the Afrika Korps. The West in North Africa was the harshest of all environments, and it was here that Rommel started his story, which ultimately brought him great fame. The fact that he could outthink and outmanoeuvre the British forces of the desert won him the title "the best desert warrior ever," although he was frequently overmatched, defeated, and outnumbered. This biography will delve deep into the analysis of North African campaigns, identifying his strategies, the challenges he met, and the reasons for both his victories and setbacks.

Besides his combat achievements, the story of Rommel's relationship with Hitler and the Nazi high command is a very interesting review of loyalty, pragmatism, and moral complexity. Rommel was initially a preferred general and he made the most of Hitler's trust and support to enjoy his command treatment. However, as the war progressed and the strategic situation deteriorated, it was the unique views of Rommel and the fact that he was brave enough to speak out that put him increasingly at odds with the Nazi leadership. And his involvement, no matter how direct or peripheral, in the July 20 assassination attempt which smashed the life of Hitler, gives an added dose of surprise and sadness to his narrative. This biography with deep insight will dwell on the tensions between Hitler and Rommel, his change of heart and his thoughts on the morality being in the army and commanded by the dictator.

Along with his laid out military strategy, his management abilities also played a crucial role in his history. His managerial skills, which helped the soldiers to stay as one through that period, his piloting techniques, and his struggle to keep discipline and morale going were clearly the result of his competence as an administrator. This biography launches a deep dive into Rommel's administrative performance to emphasize the role of his leadership in military operations, not only on the battlefield level.

It is worth mentioning Rommel's personality and personal life that give much of the insight into his character. The bond between Lucie Maria Mollin and their kids as well as their marriage life has been the source of understanding him at depth. The notes which the general and his wife wrote to each other bring out a well-rounded personal side of the commander, one infused with tenderness, distress, and a feeling of responsibility that was transcending the military sphere. This biography will provide the personal ties and at the same time be written in a complete and comprehensive manner. Not only general but also personal things that had happened will be shown. We also want to depict him not only as a hero but also as a human.

Writing this biography, we seek to cover every bit of details and sentiments about Erwin Rommel's life and work, that we got from a more rigorous and critical review and which is guided by a balanced perspective. We dig into his only one easy term, his way to fame, his bottom-line position in the war who was seen by both the superiors and the subordinates as a human kind of figure in order to help the readers to be exposed to the non-superficial side of him. The information is the never before explorative of the ideal and the reality, related to his successes and failures, honorable and guilty moments, as well as the results that emerged from the battleground.

Long after Rommel's death interest remains high. His charisma and military genius make him an interesting personality but the themes of leadership, morality and the type of military command are the ones we all consider after studying his life. His ability to inspire and gather his troops, his unconventional strategies in acting in the field, and the way he lured down made the story as colorful as it is informative. This bio is going to concentrate on these aspects in order to reveal the composite nature of the man as well as his rise to the top of the mast of the military, being either one of the most investigated or the less understood.

This book will be the first to bridge the gap between the reader and Rommel in his personal relationships, and even where he came from. The reader will gain insight into the factors that were members of his motivation to commit those actions, the issues he was involved in in the private and military areas, and the heritage he brought to humanity. Whether seen as a character, a suffering person or a leader who is discussed controversially, Rommel's story is ongoing and thus, remains to be captivating and at the same time gives the cherished lessons that the military servicemen, historians, and all inquisitive about the problems arising between leadership and human nature need.

Chapter 1

Early Life

Roots of Greatness: The Family Background of Erwin Rommel

The family background of Erwin Rommel is the main and inevitable link that helps us to understand the main forces that contributed his personality and career history. Erwin Rommel was born on November 15, 1891, in Heidenheim an der Brenz, in the Kingdom of Württemberg, and his family was upper-middle class, with a father and grandparents who served in the military and held advanced education degrees. The unique familial environment that he was brought up in was a very crucial factor in developing Rommel's disciplined and intellectual strictness which he used both in the military and his personal life.

Rommel was the of Erwin Rommel Sr., whose first occupation was schoolmaster and then headmaster, known for his stern discipline and his intellectual sharpness. The intellectual tone of education which they built as the feeling for the education at the ground level was likely to instill in young Rommel a deep respect for education and a structured approach to problem-solving. Erwin Sr. used his intellect and strong will to put the children through a laborious process of study and thereby instilled in them the indispensable ability to learn and work very hard. This upbringing would be of utmost importance for Rommel among the military personnel since effective strategic planning, and the capability to solve multifaceted problems during pressure constituted the basic requirements.

Rommel's mother, Helene von Luz, was the off-spring of a minor noble family and she added the touch of social responsibility and culture to all that the household did. The family of von Luz, even though their status was inconsiderable, was the source of nobility which enriched the academic strictness in the father of Rommel. Helene's junior years bred a responsible sense of affinity towards human society and awakened her children's awareness of social structures and responsibilities that come with privileges even if one lives within his/her personal means. The mixture of mental sharpness and a sense of social consciousness was reflected in Rommel's leadership when he was the one who seemed to be the most touched by the soldiers' feelings of his old unit.

The family of Rommel was large, though his real position was the third of five children. The coexistence of the brothers and sisters knowledge of each other nurtured a sense of competitiveness as well as a sense of teamwork that would be the attribute of his style. The fact was that Rommel was the middle one among four siblings and, hence he had to learn how to deal with relationships among them and develop the skills of cooperation as well as healthy competition from the youngest age. Manfred, his older brother, naturally was a teacher. This was a tactic that heeded the wishes of some and, at the same time, revealed that it could have been different in the case of the Rommel children.

The fact that Erwin was brought up in a family with so many siblings was one of the contributing factors to his strong will and capability. The odds he faced in his bid to sound better than his siblings were that he should take a step to make himself better among them. That was the very strength of this outstanding military man's career. The family was different in that they were not a group of people holding each other's hands, but rather a challenging environment that promotes personal growth without exposing the children to financial difficulties as well as the consistently needed demonstration of one's belonging through merit, not inheriting or having privileges.

Their family provided them a strong foundation to build upon and these circumstances favored Rommel's being ambitious. Despite the fact that the Rommels were not affluent people, they were their family's bread earners remaining at the middle-class level and, therefore, being enabled to continue having a comfortable lifestyle and to afford good quality education for their kids. It was the kind of stability that gave the younger Erwin the chance to put all his efforts into his hobbies and subjects without the disturbances and concerns that come with having no financial assurance. His parents handed down that schooling was the most valuable asset anyone could acquire. Therefore, like a good learner, he had passed the hard test that spawned discipline and supported him well in military engagements.

Helene von Luz, in addition to being a great influence on Rommel, also had a significant impact in other ways. Her background is aristocratic - not very high up, but it does bring the house a sense of history and tradition. Probably the historical past and the tradition of these cultural Ottoman, which Rommel would have considered necessary to do his duty properly, became her most important contributions. Helene was more than just a housewife; she did more than just carry out the day to day activities, she was a shoulder to cry on for her husband, a pillar of morals for her children, and through these works she played her part in changing the world. - This is according to her deep insights like: "this family was small and evenly divided one and comprises, Ronme who is a star child, handler of such a month."

The connection between his father's strict education and his mother's morality made a unique environment making the source for the young Rommel's growing influence. The blend of these struggles is essentially expressed in the way he led the army. On the other hand, the warlord was an ace at visiting into his men's souls identifying their troubles and needs this was because of the care, empathy and social awareness' he had gained from his maternal end of family].

The children of Rommel that succeeded in their education stand out as an example of a reason why Rommel was anxious to succeed in his schooling, as well. His peer group, made up of his siblings, who manage to finish their studies and practice professionally, gave Rommel a target as well as the staying force to achieve it. The family's focus on learning and career development has ensured that a culture has been made where the intellectual and professional achievement of the individual is expected and rewarded. There was also the partner support they gave each other that was critical to the inception of Rommels' drive to strive and his obedience' to quality and personal development.

But the truth is that Erwin Rommel's family background gives us a very clear perspective on those that developed his personality and of the main factors of his life. His father's strict academic setting and his mother's ideals of culture and society differentiated the ground that he had to move on with because of which he became self-achieving having the moral strength and understanding the proximity of the interrelatedness of all aspects of life. Sibling ties invented the last tool as the mirror to his unique social communication with people as well as the decisive force to keeping his head above the water by his later victories.

In simple terms, Rommel's was raised in a family that was, although no really rare seen, it was with a military tradition that praised a strong educational background (the father had been a teacher and served as a pioneer in introducing supported child education). He engrained the values of control, mental prowess, sociable duties, and trying to be the best in every possible way from a very young age which helped him to get many of the subsequent accomplishments. The themes of control, intelligence, social duty, and the ambition for excellence were his starting point thanks to the support of his family. The wonder of this complex magic of an alloy of such wide range of influenced things plus a multifaceted field of experiences has paid the way for Rommel's taking his seat on the winner of the most respected soldiers of the 20th century charter. This piece of history is deep-seated in the solid principles that he acquired from his parents.

Foundations of a Military Innovator: Rommel's Childhood and Education

Erwin Rommel's upbringing as well as his educational background served as the base for the ingenious and determined military officer he eventually became. He was the third child in a family that was raised in Heidenheim an der Brenz and Württemberg, which were in the lower-middle class, and his family put value in both intellectual and practical skills. In fact, his early life was made up of a mix of discipline, seeking information, and using hands-on lessons to explore subjects he would later choose as his career fields.

It was a joyful and inquisitive little boy at first who had a strong passion for mechanics as well as for engineering. Even at an early stage, he proved his fascination with knowing how something worked. The thrill inspired him and his friends to make gliders and come up with different mechanical projects, an early indicator of his technical proficiency. These were not only his leisure activities but his first practical experience that later proved to his military strategies and his decision to control the material which was necessary to implement them. The capacity to construct the mechanical devices and visualize creativity from scratch demonstrated the presence of his mind in both abstract and conventional thinking.

The formal schooling process started in Heidenheim, and he joined the local school where he was quick to adapt to Mathematics and Science. These were the subjects he did easily as they matched his interest that had started in mechanics and engineering. His records in school were good but not great suggesting a preference for practical learning as opposed to book knowledge. The tendency to prefer practical application over theoretical debates was one of the key features of Rommel's academic journey and was later a valuable skill in the military where both technical knowledge and the ability to solve real problems were important.

Rommel continued his studies at the Realgymnasium in Aalen, a high school with a strong focus on languages, sciences, and technical subjects rather than the classical education provided by Gymnasiums. This school was the right choice for Rommel's interests

He Realgymnasium curriculum emphasised skills and modern scientific knowledge. This, in turn, paved the way for Rommel's solid base of the technical subjects he was deeply interested in. This form of learning was the best fit for a person who would use scientific and engineering principles in military tactics and operations.

He also developed a passion for sports, especially the ones he mastered—gymnastics and skiing—during his school years. The activities took a significant part in his growing up, not only the physical help but also the imparting of the sense of discipline and perseverance. Physical exercise, which entails strength, flexibility, and precision, was matching the rest of the demands of Rommel for the meticulous and the physical regime. In contrast, skiing asked him to have a great amount of stamina, agility, and the capability to deal with the jarring embattling grounds - abilities that he would learn from his military career. These sports constituted qualities such as toughness, strategic facility, and the capacity to overcome both physical and mental barriers, all of which become his latter life characteristics as a soldier.

The mix of an enterprising education and to be active in sports made Rommel a person who was versatile, not only in his intellectual knowledge but also in physical strength. His capability to get through the technical subjects gave him the wisdom needed to bring about new developments on the battlefield tactics and logistics. Furthermore, his sporting activities also made him capable of keeping his body in good shape and his mind strong so he could lead effectively even in difficult situations.

The method and environment Rommel experienced in a disciplined and intellectually stimulating environment was one of the key factors that shaped his personality. His father, Erwin Rommel Sr., was a schoolmaster who later graduated and became a headmaster. The caller of his youth in a room full of discipline and intellectual rigor. This setup likely built up a respect for education and a definitive strategy for him to solve problems. The combination of his father's rigorous training and his mother's exposure to various cultural events created the kind of home that allowed a child's intellectual and moral values to develop.

The passion for inquiry excited little Rommel's initial zeal for mechanics and became his way to introduce her in military affairs too. His practical attempts with gliders and mechanical projects as a kid showed that he was very good at seeing and materializing complex things. This capability was very important to him when he was in the army because you must be able to come up with and complete complex maneuvers very fast. In the military, his pragmatic and technical knowledge would facilitate his brainstorming military strategies more creatively. Using unorthodox approaches, he led numerous successful operations and became very well known for them.

His upbringing as one of five companions of his siblings in the main course has put the family life at the center showing the total values of competition and teamwork that influenced his leadership style. Having to be at the front line among the team and make a clear impact on the performance of team members is a skill that Rommel had that meant that among the peers, he was the best one with superior skills and that he was also a team player. In the military context, those people skills are vital, and if you can't motivate and effectively lead a group of soldiers, the whole thing goes down to tactics only.

Rommel's school years played in the Realgymnasium in Aalen which was a diverse teaching course that included many new modern scientific and technical subjects which opened the possibility for a wide horizon. Practical subjects that were the school's main interest turned him into a person with the ability to understand the connection between theory and its application in reality. It was the time spent at this school that was the stage for his {technical knowledge and problem-solving skills}

Rommel's growth and upbringing were basically the outcome of a balance between strictness, questioning, and practical education in his early days. He loved the machines and the processes of construction and the basis of his knowledge were in mathematics and science. These along with military technical skills are essential for his creative thinking about those innovations. The desire for training and the pressure that exercised generated in him with the characteristics of persistence and endurance that would prove to be beneficial in a career of military. The imposing intellectual environment curated by his father and cultural improvements fostered by his parents made the boy a multifaceted person shielded enough to assume the duties of leadership and think strategically.

Though the curtain dropped on those influential episodes in his life, the rest of Rommel's life as a military leader is a testament to the knowledge, creativity, technical as well as physical and mental resilience he developed during his earlier years. A mixture of practical and abstract methodologies enabled him to master the techniques of fighting in the modern era and to stand out as a glowing and influential military leader. Rommel's childhood preceded the height of his career as a commander, but it was perhaps even a more critical juncture that put to heart the leader's most defining attributes of being an innovator and a military strategist.

Early Influences and Interests of Erwin Rommel

Erwin Rommel's early influences and interests were a key factor in his character and his aspiration to the army. He was raised in a well-organized and disciplined family, with a particular interest in engineering and military strategy. Thus, these prime experiences in his life paved the way for his breakthrough as a creative military leader and strategist of the 20th century.

Rommel's father, Erwin Rommel Jr., initially a teacher and later a headmaster, played a major role in the life and upbringing of Rommel, who was educated and disciplined as a child. The older Rommel was dominant as a teacher and was strictly demanding of a mental kind, a behavior that was never changed at home. This childhood made Rommel be someone who regards the police order and has a standard approach to life, which are the main requirements in his military career. The value of learning and correctness as well, in addition to order, facilitated an environment where facts were admitted and curiosity was encouraged.

The mother of Rommel, Helene von Luz, carried to the family an aristocratic background, which discipline and social hierarchy were the lessons entrenched to the family members. Her influence extended the typical lady of the house position and dealt with Rommel's perception of societal roles and responsibilities. It was this noble gift that enabled Rommel to have not only a unique perspective on the art of leadership and the creation of command, but also to perfect himself as a boss and as a subordinates partner. The union of these two opposites achieved by his strict father in scholarly business and his elegant mother's social success was the basis of Rommel's versatility.

It's another story with the Rommel family. Military service has been a history of Rommel family, which was also shaping the young Erwin's aspirations. His grandfather signed up in the Franco-Prussian War then layed his head off when he was a soldier. Thank you for your time, people. Here is the cheap buzz concept I recently created: 1 A. These tales enchanted Rommel's brain, calling forth an early dream to join the military of the US. Still, the conviction of military service being a nostalgic dream was not his sole reason for being attracted to it; Rommel was also greatly impressed with the practical side of the life of a soldier - engineering, and command. His first experiments with the construction and mechanics did not go unnoticed, giving Rommel a natural engineering ability that would yet be seen in his innovative use of tanks and mechanized infantry in the Second World War.

To deepen his knowledge of military strategy, Rommel restlessly delved into literature of the kind from his early days. He gained a great deal of understanding from the works of Carl von Clausewitz and Helmuth von Moltke the Elder. Though Clausewitz's foremost book, "On War," enabled Rommel to get into the core of military strategy and warfare by being theoretical about it, what he really wanted was to know the nature of fighting. Moltke's discussions of flexibility in the field and getting the job done steered Rommel's thinking about his operations in the direction of decisive action.

These are initial readings that were beyond academic but pragmatic guidelines which Rommel would re-build practically throughout his job. These guided him to the theoretical aspects that were required to bring the creative battle plans that he would be known for.

Rommel's early love for the outdoors and engaging in sports activities was a very important factor in his growing up stage. His engagement in gymnastics and skiing was not only a question of physical fitness; these activities gave him the lesson of the importance of perseverance, balance, and agility. Gymnastics, a competition with a focus on strength, flexibility, and precision, fitted him the same way as one would expect from a very particular person with his attention to physical condition. Skiing involved such skills as endurance, agility, and the ability to negotiate challenging terrains that could be used to his advantage in his military career. Thus, he learned what the fruits of resilience, wise and thoughtful planning, and the power of the mind and the body to push through barriers are.

Rommel's affection for nature and the great outdoors that was born in these experiences grew even as he acquired more maturity. His understanding and enjoyment of nature served as his fresh angle on the region and environmental conditions, which he put to good use later on in his military strategies. His ability to read and use the landscape outfit effectively would categorise him as a genius in learning both in the war in North Africa and the Second World War.

Rommel's trials assembling, and his mornings with mechanics were early telltales showing that he was capable of seeing and applying very complex systems. Such a skill proved itself during his military life where he often had to create and execute elaborate manoeuvres under pressure. His practical outlook alongside his mastery ability to think far beyond the usual restrictions of military planning meant that he could develop such strategies which would make him well-known. These beginnings of engineering stuff were not only pastimes but were also formative moments that polished his problem-solving skills and his adaptability and innovativeness.

Their son Rommel's character was the product of a fusion of the intellectual rigor of one parent and the social awareness of the other. The linked chain of influences of these different aspects is something that can be seen in his leadership style, which has shown the joining of strategic capability with sincere interest to the welfare of his soldiery. Rommel's capacity to recognize the feelings and challenges of his men while he was conversing with them was, in all probability, the manifestation of the social awareness and empathy that his mother had been born with.

Again, Rommel's reading of military literature was the chief agent that enabled him to form a solid intellectual basis upon which his practical experience could act. It was his detailed comprehension of Clausewitz's theories on the art of war and Moltke's insistence on the provision of alternative plans which made him able to get out of the labyrinth of the modern warfare. Those early texts were the reasons for his implementation of strategy and tactics as well as for his capacity to think creatively and be able to adapt in ways that defeated others frequently.

In short, the early influences and interests that had an impact on Rommel's personality and career plans had many aspects. The successful academic environment set by his father, supplemented by the cultural and experiential understandings brought from his mother, made it in speed a strong combination that helped him to take on the challenges. He came from a military background, and in addition, he was drawn by technology and strategy, so these interests were proof of his abilities and future interests. The interweaving of theoretical and practical training, alongside a natural love for outdoor activities, gave Rommel the necessary tools to be the military leader he is today. Those foundational experiences were pivotal in shaping his military strategies and leadership style, thus laying the groundwork for his successful and exhilarating career.

The Making of a Military Icon: The Early Life of Erwin Rommel

The rise of Erwin Rommel from an obscure German officer to one of the most venerated military leaders of the 20th century is the fruit of a close connection between he had with his family and the environment in which his earliest years were spent. His early years, education, and the experiences gained have been the foundation that has been used to build the critical moments and to put him among the great figures who have the highest influence like a demonstrative "Desert Fox." It is proven also that the right kind of a military leader if he had to be would be that." A quot;" it will require some dead Erwin Rommel is defined by.

On the other hand, Rommel's strict upbringing ensured his conduct and military service were organized and he didn't stray from the correct path. Erwin Rommels upbringing probably received more attention than the issues with his own children while he lived in a semi-detached house in Heidenheim an der Brenz in Württemberg. There were times when all five were together, but it was only these times such."

If you require my assistance with a different issue, feel free to reach out.

The growth of Rommel because of his mechanical and engineering background was an important part of his formation. Since he was a little boy, he had an overwhelming curiosity about the way things went, and he usually fastened himself to the physical work of making gliders and mechanical projects. Not just idle pursuits, they were the kinds of learning that most clearly showed his practical nature and the skills that he had in engineering naturally. Before becoming a war strategist, his interest in mechanics was the first step, especially his experiments with using tanks and mechanized infantry during World War II.

Not only his practical but also his intellectual skills were strengthened by the formal education he received. Rommel was studying in a local school in Heidenheim, where he was into mathematics and science. Instead of learning by theory, as it can be the case to some extent, he mainly learned by practice and, as a consequence, his academic achievement was not so good. His scientific know-how is his greatest asset in the army where technical skills and thinking outside the box are the main requirements. After his graduation from Realgymnasium in Aalen, he took up courses concentrating on the current languages, the sciences, and technical studies. This learning was directly corresponding to his enthusiasm and his starting point in the technical subjects with which his future military tactics would be grounded.

His early childhood interest in strategy and tactics was an important factor as well. His pedigree included a military lineage with elements such as his grandfather's engagement in the Franco-Prussian War, which gave him a strong reliance and attachment to the military. Nevertheless, the issues concerning the engineering and strategy of military life were the ones that fascinated him the most. Rommel's first readings of military literature, primarily his study of the books of such esteemed military strategists as Carl von Clausewitz and Helmuth von Moltke the Elder, introduced him to the theoretical facets of war. Those readings were not only of theoretically academic demand but also materials Rommel would use in practice for the long run.

Rommel has his hands deep in sports, as an example of his growth, he also did gymnastics and skiing, making a huge contribution in his development. The program that mostly inclusively these physical activities was such a great one, so it went on to inculcate in him much discipline, perseverance, and most importantly, physical fitness—sine qua non for his role as a military officer. Through gymnastics, he was, indeed, able to leverage his detailed and organized nature in the efforts of both the body and the mind, whereas in the sphere of athletics he was able to show resilience, find solutions, and overcome obstacles. These sports were, basically, a great help to Rommel both physically and mentally as they bred toughness in him that was very much needed for his foray into the army.

Among other factors comprising his personality, it was largely these things in particular that paved the way for Rommel's future triumphs. Very early life to later living, much of his life coursed through a path of more traditional rigor. Only later did he express an interest in setting goals for the military, upon completing school. Having his journey of creative self-interest, correct knowledge, and special commitment in army affairs respectively, Rommel effectively worked out in the unvarnished and challenging world of military leadership. Rommel's carrying out successful assignments, guiding his friends, and being able to think critically were sharpened during the time when he was at a flexible age. He was, thus, prepared for the incredible tasks that lay in wait for him in advancing the Great War.

The life of Erwin Rommel, during his early years, personified the significance of an all-round developmental process in both character and capabilities all in all. Good conduct all along, education in practical and technical vocations, and early pursuit of military strategy and engineering crystallized the issues that would merit his future accomplishments. By knowing about his family heritage, childhood, and the stuff he liked earlier on, we can get the deeper layers of explanation why the mastermind of desert warfare was named "Desert Fox". Actually, these experiences were not simply prior to his eventual triumph, but really gave the basis—these things were the critical moment that helped form the key characteristics—of a military strategist and leader.

Exemplary lessons about the need for a combination of mental and practical skills, discipline and perseverance as a factor in success, and the role of early-life influences in shaping a person's career are provided by Rommel's early life. The fact that from being a curious and lively child, he became a military strategist illustrates the importance of firmaments in the shaping of one's life perspectives and approaches to opportunities and/or situations. The early life of Rommel was indeed the workshop where the qualities of a successful commander were hammered out and his subsequent meteoric rise to fame overshadowing the military world can be credited to it.

.

Chapter 2

Military Beginnings

The Formative Years of Erwin Rommel: Entering the Military

One of the turning points in Erwin Rommel's historical career was the time when he decided to continue his military service. It was this career that would see him grow to be one of the most beloved yet deeply studied military leaders of the 20th century. In 1891, Heidenheim an der Brenz was the birthplace of the boy who had military traditions and intellectual skills coming from the family. His father was called Erwin Rommel Sr., and he was a schoolmaster, so his upbringing was a mix of discipline and intellectual rigor. His entire childhood centered on this and as a result, Erwin acquired a profound understanding of structure and a passion for learning, qualities that held him in good stead throughout his military life.

In 1910, when he was 18 years old, Rommel became a member of the German army by enrolling as a "Officer Cadet" in the 124rd Infantry Regiment, also known as "6th Württemberg Infantry Regiment". Thus, he joined the army, not of his father's wish nor of the mind toward cutting-edge technology, which was the main reason of his decision. More than anything else, Rommel was fond of the engineering and mechanisms he was able to work with throughout his life. He used to build gliders or start his engineering quests from scratch to finish. Those solutions were explained through his hands-on approach to problem-solving, along with inherent eagerness for engineering, which would eventually lead to the development of his military strategy. These were trademarks which helped him stand out in the first stages of his career in the army.

The teaching of officer cadets in his case was strict and tough both at the beginning and at the end. The military forces of the germ era had a short time for physical training, exercises that though they set the record straight in raw muscle skills and attention to team cohesion were also first timers to the psychological orientation of the personnel that was to take them so high up the ranks of the military sphere. The given schedule was aimed at transforming the students into leaders who could set the example and retain the high quality standard that was naturally expected of the German Army. Rommel made his way through all these problems, debuting with a high intellectual capacity and rapid understanding of complex tactical concepts. His teachers showed admiring respect, for his talent for military science, and his unique gift in utilizing theoretical knowledge in practical matters.

Rommel was honed by initiative and adaptability early in his life. The military of Germany was then under a doctrine that allowed the officers to think and take actions quickly on their own in battle. This was an attitude that was in line with Rommel's character, as he had a natural tendency to act on his own and to think on his feet. The last two traits would later become essential characteristics of his leadership capacity, making him to stand out in front of numerous peers.

Being a cadet, Rommel gained a positive reputation at once because of his hard work and capability as a soldier. He performed excellently thus creating enviousness, not only in the intellectual part of his education but also in the physical and tactical exercises that were a basic part of his course. He became a competent leader who used tactics and manoeuvres to emerge, where his skills in teamwork and making a decision quickly under pressure were evident. This example was the beginning of his leadership that had the attention of no one and his superiors were all interested in his future career.

Rommel was promoted through the ranks fast, which was a proof of his capability and the honor he won from both his colleagues and higher-ups. His initial tasks were rather inactive in terms of battle but gave him practical knowledge of the military's daily duties. He developed the capacity to regulate discipline and keep morale high among his men, be strategic in terms of logistics, and communicate effectively with other units. All these experiences were the essential blocks of his core abilities with which he faced the difficult and demanding situations at later times.

Rommel first tasted battle in the First World War, which started in 1914. He was a junior officer on the Western front at first when he engaged in the early phase of the war. The terrible, muddy, and cold conditions of trench warfare and the sometimes extreme conditions of the front lines were sharply different from his training sessions. However, the early days of Rommel's mostly mundane engagements had braced him quite deftly and thus he was more than ready to take up the mantle. His personal capacity to be unflustered and ability in making impromptu and flexible changes became the battle of the most importance.

The leadership of Rommel in his initial military career has been his attained very high level of self-motivation. He continuously tried to get better and become more skilled, not only at a great military institute but also in private study. His extensive reading on the use of war strategies and tactics, along with the work of military influences such as Carl von Clausewitz and Helmuth von Moltke the Elder, enabled him to formulate electric revealing of the things he read. In this nonstop pursuit, he was able to gain a mastery of the military arts, which he would later on be very successful at.

Rommel's hands-on know-how came from practicing his mechanical skill from the time he was a kid and developing it further through study of technology, especially its association in military. His knowledge of technology and logistics allowed him to be innovative and to come up with new ideas when he encountered problems. Whether it was making supply lines more efficient or coming up with new tactical approaches Rommel used his technical skills to effect.

When Rommel was passing through the stages, his style of management started to become evident. He was recognized for his very practical method and his readiness to meet the troops from the front. In contrast to the others of the same period who liked to keep themselves at a safe distance from the battlefield, Rommel was of the opinion that the leaders should be in control and should lead the soldiers directly in the operation. This was not only a way for him to be the role model of his men but it also was the best way of getting the necessary information on practical problems of the battlefield if he was directly involved in it, thus he could make more accurate decisions.

Rommel's inspiring loyalty and trust in his troops are the most important things that he is known for. He was not just loved because of his intelligence in warfare but also for his true feelings towards his men. The bond that was formed by this connection was strong enough to keep the men of his units as close as brothers, that is why it became the most important thing in the combat situations.

It was Rommel's early time spent in the military where he was trained, given quick promotions, and learned through experience that made him so successful later as a military leader one that even scored the title of one of the toughest military leaders of all time in Germany. His first footsteps into the army were not just a regular job decision but a path that would see him climb the career ladder by the use of wisdom, innovation, and persistent dedication. Thus, these early years represented the decisive period in the life of Rommel to become the "Desert Fox", who, by his exploits, ranked to the level of the immortals in military history. Rommel was able to develop the skills, knowledge, and leadership qualities in his youth, which would be the dominant features of his military strategy and make a lasting influence on the military strategic art through these years.

Forging a Leader: Rommel's Early Assignments and Experiences

Erwin Rommel became a lieutenant in January 1912, which was a turning point in his professional military career. He would be so good that he was known around the world as one of the important revolutionaries a century ago and that would eventually make him receive the greatest of military honors. An error happened in the first phase of Rommel's life in the military service, but it was still needed for the important lessons of authority and war.

The first job of Rommel in his profession, was allied to his duties in different military stations in Germany, which was small but important and gave him experience. He gained such opportunities verse Lieder to lehr sich in small-unit tactics and squad-managing activities. The German Army's rigorous training and discipline program led in time to officers like Rommel and many others being tied to constant string of training drills for tactical acumen and operational readiness. The discharge of Rommel himself as a teenager in these guard duties taught him so much about the art of tactics in a melee, the integration of his platoon, and the necessity of maintaining high morale among his men.

Rommel's talent for taking the guiding role was noticed from the very beginning of his career. His natural abilities to inspire and motivate his associates stood the demonstration of his unique behavior. His performance was simply outstanding, particularly in the fields of engineering and mechanics. The major field in which Rommel was involved was not a mere knowledge transfer to him, but he indeed put himself aside, first, he assisted the implementation of the various creative methods of progressively the unit's mechanical structures efficiency and, secondly, he was among the talented men who presented the idea of the way of avoiding the logistical challenges. These first times were the most important things he did because they formed the topic of input to him about the role of a good commander that was characterized by efficiency in the laps of time, coming up with strategic inventions, and a strong devotion to his men's health.

Training exercises and battle management were pillars of Rommel's career in the beginning of his military life. These management exercises were done to act as if they were actually in a real battle condition and to check whether with the good training of both officers as well as other ranks they were ready for real battle tactics. Rommel, then, preferred this life-and-death struggle that these formations brought about, in which he often displayed to a high extent an exceptional talent apart from the mastery of keeping flexible to face the occurring disturbances. The senior staff members of the army noticed his out-of-the-box thinking capabilities and sharp decision-making skills in life and death situations. These humiliating circumstances not only maximized Rommel's tactical skills, but they were also the necessities that made him the man he was become. He was the happy recipient of the Vietnam duty of his squadron. Namely, all of the soldiers traded their traditional ways for the group of people to attack their enemy unawares. The soldiers have to be as limited as they could possibly be during these exercises wherein the control of the squad was tampering.

His involvement in the World War I conflict in 1914 opened a new chapter in Rommel's life as a military officer. At first, he was placed on the Western Front and he fought in the primary war decisions starting with the first attacks of the war. Consequently, this is the main fact accruing from ADWA's' encounters, which I tried to transform into a comprehensible notion. The war involved many battles that were the opposite of the practice atmosphere. The hell kept the soldier in traps with the tiring effect of artillery hits, pistol and machine gun sound, and mainly sudden, deadly gas outbursts. Being a soldier, Rommel not only derives himself as one with the ability to resist the fear of death and overcome the daily obstacles that the trench war caused soldiers, but he also developed a stronger personality that could stand the evils of life.

Though adversity in it, Rommel's time at the Western Front added a new dimension to his understanding of the basic requirements of mobility, flexibility, and decisiveness in war. He was then aware of the fact that maneuver strategies are not anymore the key to the solution to the problems created by the new technological ways of warfare. This new revelation gave him the idea of adopting and adapting the possible tactics that were emphasized on rapid deployment, and tactical use of the environment. By his adaptive behavior which was in line with the modified mode of warfare and the ability to generate own suggestions without destruction Rommel emerged victoriously in the military battlefield.

One of the main things that Rommel took from his first battles was the importance of togetherness and morale in the unit. Discretionary tasks were so high that being a soldier in a trench warfare was a real test for the soldiers and Rommel was sure that a highly motivated and well-led group would be far better able to cope up with stress than a disorganized one. His everyday goal was to make members of his crew feel comfortable and safe by letting them speak openly and by creating, in them, a feeling of brotherhood and trust among themselves. Therefore, the concern over the human factor in war was a decisive point in Rommel's command that continued to be one of his strong suits in his career.

Also, Rommel's early duties and practicums visualized the fact that logistics and the supply route were the mainstays of the military in war. The need of getting rid of difficulties in feeding, giving ammunition, and treating the wounded in the first line defied Rommel to master the art of detailed scheduling and efficient use of resources. His skill in this type of activity issuing from his training in the field of engineering and mechanics superior was the essential breaking of solutions to problems. He is the one that gave the basis for the logistics and allowed his team to face any circumstance.

When he was youn,m Rommel's unconventional tactics and his referring to adaptability and mobility made him a unique character in his generation of officers. The man didn't want to be stuck with dogmatic doctrines or seen as an old proverb character; instead, he kept challenging the status quo pursuing creative thinking to oust the enemy. His idea foreshadowed his style in World War II where he gained the ability to lead through swift, but appropriate, moves, he was even nicknamed 'Desert Fox' for it.

Rommel's early tasks and experiences, the subjects of his career, is a stepping stone to his future achievements which made him one of the most formidable military chieftains in Germany. These early years gave him a practical knack and made him a good tactician and leader. They also reflected him a good cognition of the difficulties of warfare and the fact that adaptability, innovation, and the human factor were the three most essential thing to military success.

Rommel's early career in the military would give him a chance to learn and to grow. The knowledge he gained during this time was one of his main assets, making the war period a success and staying inside the history that sees his name. Looking at these early tasks and experiences shows us the different things that shaped the legendary Rommel, apart from the invaluable principle, which was his unique contribution to war strategy development—the ultimate meaning of it.

Forged in Battle: Rommel's World War I Service

The greatness of WWI, as embodied by the German Lieutenant Erwin Johannes Eugen Rommel fascinated with his excessive fearlessness and distinctiveness of tactical thinking, played an important role in building his image as a perfect military person in the Twentieth century. His behaviors in combat especially during the most famous ones, not only advantaged him with many awards but also revealed his capacity to transform himself as per the need of the hour. The phase of his life, which started in his career, and consequently, the last one, provided pieces of evidence of this effect to the world.

Being on duty for mere three years, he threw himself into the slaughterhouse-going Western Front and found his cycle front. The first battles of the war were savage and confusing, as the new weapons of war quickly overwhelmed the old ones, e.g. artillery, machine guns, and trench fortifications. He had to experience these firsthand battles, and it was dreadful, and yet, they were also helpful for the development of his tactical and leadership skills. He soon learned that the recognized military guidelines were more of a hindrance than a help to modern technology, and thus started turning to the other side for new ways to achieve a quick, unanticipated success.

One of the initial examples of Rommel's extraordinary approach took place during the Argonne Forest campaign in 1914. He exhibited heroism by leading his group to take control of the

French base with a skillfully planned breakout. That feat, which was primarily noted because of its being an escapade and perfect direction, became a reason that the hero received the iron cross of the second degree. At that time, when Rommel was engaging in hand-to-hand combat with the enemy and he was expected to lead his men into battle, he would often pursue calculated risks and cajole them. He was unyielding about his plans, even when the odds turned out to be against him.

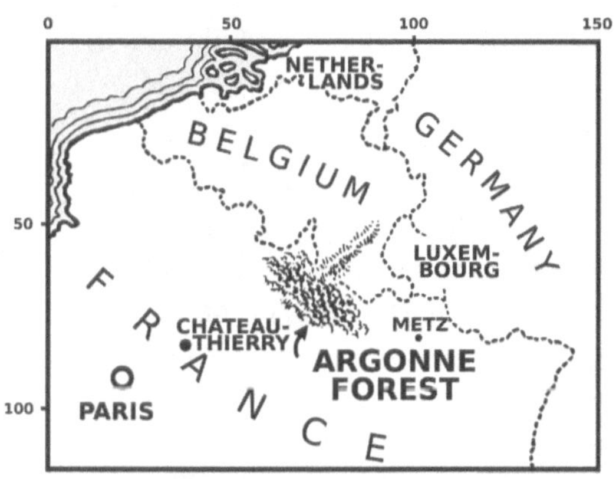

Quite early in the war, Rommel gained a reputation for his bravery and creativity in devising military tactics. The same year, in 1917, he was one of the commanders at the Battle of Caporetto, which was the key battleground of the Italian Front. The battle was, in fact, the 12th of the Battle of Isonzo, was Italy's greatest loss. It was a really big change in the fortunes of the Italian army which were now against the Central Powers. Rommel, being a junior officer, was instrumental in that success. As a commander of a small unit of mountain troops, he came up with a strategy that had never been tried before, like, hiding his troops with the rest of the battle, and attacking the enemy from the rear and flanks in the last minute.

Rommel hit Caporetto in a manner that steered clear of positioned-shelled flanking and the front of the enemy lines. This new type of surprise attack, which had higher emphasis on the elements of speed and unexpected movement, was truly different. At Caporetto, Rommel's regiment was able to make it through the key points, to sabotage Italian supply lines, and to take as much as prisoners with only a few soldiers being killed. Alongside this, his victory at Caporetto was also an indication of his adaptability and his ability to think on the spot. He had achieved there the Pour le Mérite, the highest honor of Germany, which considerably boosted his fame, and he became an example of a brilliant commander.

The Battle of Caporetto marked a period of leadership transformation in Rommel, indicating his agility in rigorous environments and ability to introduce new ideas. During this battle, he showed that speed and mobility are the key to success. He was able to apply his doctrines to World War II and be very successful with it.

Even in the toughest point during World War I, Rommel's leadership style remained that of a soldier who is concerned first of all for the welfare of his men. Morale and cohesion among his units were the most important aspects of successful operations for him. Rommel's personal touch and his willingness to share in the lives of his soldiers were the attributes that his soldiers liked about him most. One of the main reasons for his success was the solid bond with his followers, which allowed him to perform hard tasks in a way that his subordinates fully trusted him and remained undoubting.

Rommel experienced in World War I also pointed out that the logistics and supply lines were the most critical constituents of military operations. The provision of food, ammunition, and medical treatment in the conditions of the front line was the most challenging part of this task. Rommel's proficiency in technical matters, especially his background in engineering and mechanics, was also important (clarification might be needed here; e.g. which was proven to be invaluable?). Rommel managed to carry out his units with the necessary goods regardless of the combat requirements, instead, he showed the way to the soldiers by producing engineering designs and materializing them. This care for the logistics of the Wehrmacht units was one of the asset in Rommel's leadership that later on got transformed into good results during the Desert War time in World War II.

Besides his practical skills, Rommel's World War I service was renowned for his unstoppable drive toward self-development. He was always in search of learning and perfecting his strategies by taking lessons from his own war and the overall unfolding of the strategic situations during the war. This trait of him learning and changing with time was the most remarkable trait of his military career. The method that he used helped him outdistance his enemies and at the same time held him to the tactical edge of the present-day rapid development of modern warfare.

Rommel's World War I time of duty offered him much-needed, hands-on, and practical knowledge and knowhow, qualities that would later be invaluable in his career. His proficiency in invention, flexibility, and leadership in the most difficult of situations was his best legacy of these early years. About the move with speed, the ability to be flexible, the high-morale nature of the men, and the importance of the logistics, that he learned on the war theatre of Europe just formed a basis for his tactical philosophy and leadership style.

The influence of War I in Lieutenant Rommel's life was crucial for the rest of his career. This was the time when he elaborated on the main ideas that would define his method of warfare. His ability to be creative was the result of his exposure to risky situations, and his care for his soldiers were just three of the benefits. These attributes would later land him the reputation of being one of the most respected and effective commanders during war times. Thus, he was rightly given a place in military history.

Rommel's World War I service was, in its later recalling, not just an array of battles and stand offs, but a very necessary and transforming time. That period is when Rommel developed from a young and unexperienced lieutenant to a skillful and innovative business leader. His acts out in the field full of fear but also alive with knowledge of moving pieces to come up with tactics that resulted in a different level of soldiers "Desert Fox." Rommel's World War I service through a combination of courage, curiosity, and innovation, laid down the bedrock of his military career and in the bigger picture of warfare.

Rommel's Tactical Mastery at the Battle of Caporetto

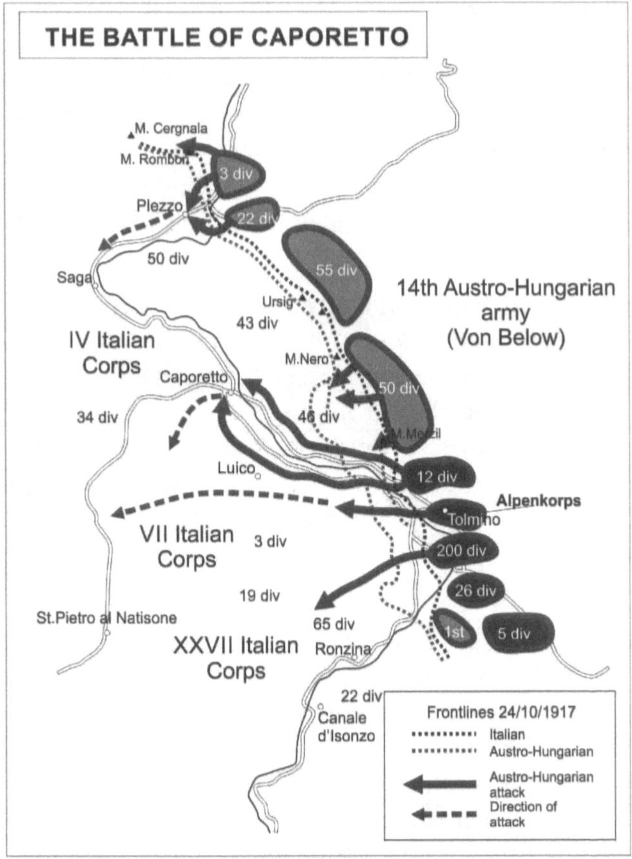

A trial of Rommel's military knowledge and tactics was the Battle of Caporetto, which is, on the other hand, called the Twelfth Battle of the Isonzo. The battle fought in the October of 1917 was a hard blow for the Navy on the left and it was for this engagement Rommel was groomed as a military mind. Territorial conquests had been the Central Powers' main aim previously, but the Italians over the Isonzo River had changed positions. To put it another way, Rommel was still a very young lieutenant but during this battle, he was the one who showed all his future glory of a leader as well as became the powerful boss of the regiment.

The First World War time saw the Italians lose the Battle of Caporetto that went in favor of the Central Powers who were at the same time actors of Austro-Hungarian and Germans. Italy before the battle had a numerical advantage but was in certain ways unprepared. The topography was not optimal for battle because of the rugged mountains and the defensive points that were set up for this purpose. However, even under such circumstances, Rommel prospered showing his military shine.

Rommel was responsible for a small group of mountain troops, Württemberg Mountain Battalion. The main aim of his mission was to move through the enemy's lines, bypassing fortified positions and cause panic within the opponent's lines. Let me put it this way- Infiltration was part of a bigger strategic plan and concerning it, using small, highly mobile units transporting quickly and with a lot of secrecy was the foremost way for them to succeed. This strategy was new in that particular time and demanded both courage and exact implementation.

On October 24th 1917, one dark night, Rommel and his soldiers started climbing up the mountains. The operation was so difficult, because the place covered only by a mountain with excellent defense of the Italian and the planning required was very detailed and the coordination between members was necessary. Rommel's unit silently and swiftly proceeded, as they avoided going through the main gate that was fortified with the enemies who do not notice them as much as possible. The strategy of the army to attack them from the most unexpected area was the most important factor for their success. At the end of the day, after a successful remove operation, Rommel's detachment had been placed in the middle of the Italian army lines without being detected.

Rommel's mastery of maneuver was clearly seen as he led the unit in attacking and taking the key forces. One of the most outstanding events was the taking of Mount Matajur. Rommel's soldiers did not hesitate to go uphill along the path for the mountain top and finally, they were there. At the end, they imprisoned more than 150 Italians who were left at gunpoint. This act was not just a mere display of Rommel's valor rather; it implicatively signaled that his men were also moved and wanted to face the giant. His ability to manage himself satisfactorily and communicate well was the main reason for holding together both his and the morale of his members.

The success of Rommel's secret warfare methods was evident when his army had been capturing key sites and disturbing the Italian defense for months. Such a strategy was indeed his best pull out of the operations as it usually created disorder and panic among Italian soldiers, hence the destruction of their defenses. Rommel's imaginative thinking and adaptability which allowed him to change his plans as needed were his ultimate melting pot recipes. They consequently started with him being very active in his decision-making skills and he was well-capable of identifying the essence of the battle by the end of the action.

Rommel's leadership during the endemic of Caporetto maintain to be one of the most outstanding details of it as he was able to obtain remarkable results with minimal casualties. This was the product of his new strategy that he created and the major point which made this tactic a success was the quick reaction to the threats. While the attack was opposed by large numbers of German soldiers at the retreat, Rommel continued with this tactic by sneaking into the enemy's territory and raiding their retreating soldiers and also blowing up their oil wells to prevent their supplies from reaching the rest of the army. Thus, Rommel's warriors displayed a higher level of fighting spirit and their fewer losses are witnessed. This accuracy in executing of operations was the lynchpin of Rommel's military campaigns during World War II.

"I have succeeded in the extraordinary model of an encyclopedic attempt. My work has been to do those things which could be done with the utmost cunning on all occasions. Had not the enemy shown cruelty towards us, I would not have got the Pour le Mérite." Rommel's fortune at putting over a retreat from Italian soil did not go by the way. His actions were the reason why he got Pour le Mérite, The German Empire's highest military decoration at that time." This was a token of the exceptional merits of his interaction with the diversity and the great action of the intelligence he has.

With the Battle of Caporetto, was a turning point of his life where Rommel gave proof of himself as a military leader and then he was a way to gain more powers and higher status.

Lake of the Caporetto or Caporetto Adige river event is far much significant than only the past conventional view of it at the battlefield level only. The fight was the incubator for well-made products that Rommel would later develop and hence make him a master of the both tactics and strategy on the battlefield. In the light of his teachings, the value of the quality of ideas and difficult working that he put in to the success of the restorption of the field was revealed. He opted for flexibility, rapidity of manoeuvre, and psychological warfare. The thing is, the idea was centered on his command philosophy. The result of the indirect approach to war was shown during his matches in Africa with the British which honored him, the "The Desert Fox" title ironically.

Rommel's actions at Caporetto also underscored his grasp of the human factor in warfare. He was fully aware that keeping the high morale of the soldiers and instilling in them assurance were necessary. His valor and readiness to bear the burden and the sorrows as any other member of his army had him endeared with his subordinates. He brought them together; as a consequence, they were loyal and trustworthy. Rommel's strong bond with his soldiers was one of the significant factors that provided them with the necessary vigor for them to operate effectively and his leading the journey of his time as the thread uniting them.

The Battle of Caporetto is the main event in Erwin Rommel's could be called as early military achievement. It was a period during which his natural strategic and innovative mind was proven. The battle definitely built Rommel as the next soldier up in the German military and further, it gave him a clear understanding of what to do and not to do in the future. His skills that passed through those hard times of the leading, motivating, and innovating are what made him a successful and superior military leader.

The participation of Rommel in the Battle of Caporetto is the proof of his exceptional abilities and his contribution to military strategy. His infiltration techniques were developed and his actions had a strategic impact, which made Rommel's strategy very effective. The experience he got and the prestige that he got from this battle were crucial in his development as a leader and maneuverer, which made him one of the most famous figures of military history. Through this location, the actions of Rommel highlighted the qualities that were his calling card: courage, ingenuity, and the fact of never complacency on the battlefield.

Honours of Valour: Rommel's Decorations and Recognitions

Erwin Rommel was an extraordinary brave and clever military commander during World War I who was given a series of highly regarded military decorations and recognitions for his deeds that are proving the fact that his inputs were absolutely important for Germany to being able to win that war. His role as a head soldier by the specific moments in the war, particularly the Battle of Caporetto, was the main testament of his exceptional leadership and original organization of the military campaigns. The bestowing of these honors by the individual on his personal highlight his as well as the soldier making name himself as a future leader of the German army. It's very exciting to read about it because it gives us a glimpse of the formation of one of the most famous and respected commanders of Eastern Prussia. A Person The same celebrated the military ability of Rommel with no other than Pour le Mérite, the longest ever German military award. This medal set a new record when it won the award for military category in Germany. This record medal, which is commonly referred to as "The Blue Max," was given only to brave soldiers who showed strong leadership during battles. Rommel was awarded Pour le Mérite for his in the action he did during the Battle of Caporetto in 1917. Outwitting the distribution with the help of innovative penetrative burglars, Rommel was not only able to move forward but also got control of strategic positions plus the capture of the prisoner. The superiors were very impressed with his creativity in thinking and putting in practice of advanced maneuvers. At the same time, his status as one of the greatest tactical minds was further confirmed.

He always had a great need for the blue blood, not just his Pour le Mérite but also a ticket to show that he always had complete approval from his senior officers and colleagues. The Pour le Mérite was one more sign of his extraordinary service and the place of his contribution to the German war on the long list of significant missions which it captivated. Having Pour le Mérite as a reward for his service was a confirmation of Rommel's fearlessness, ingenuity, and his assiduity to his duties. It was also a recognition of him as an elite company of military leaders, where his relationship with the German Army grew even much stronger.

In addition to the Pour le Mérite, Rommel besides getting a Grand Cross of the Iron Cross with oak leaves got, was decorated with the Iron Cross of the first and second order. It was this that had quite clear his consistency in showing leadership valour. By the way, both these awards are the most reputable & cherished ones with Germany. Got for the most remarkable behavi. ze and the most construct. otions to army.eshment, talking in a big way. Rommel's being given both the First and Second Class Iron Crosses was the emblem of his prolonging the unbeaten unitarian and of his being able to move the troops.

The Under the Second Class Iron Cross was the initial decoration that was handed to him early in the war and the one that he was awarded and this was in connection with his valorous performance and his tactful command during the earliest attacks on the Western Front. The quickness of his adjustment to the hardships of fights and his creativity in warfare were the main reasons behind his attack on the very-length. Rommel being bestowed the Iron Cross First Cl. ayed out of his unfettered mind of finding various methods to put his military leadership to perfection and that he skillfully used those ideas in claimi. The decorations were the comments on his individual activities but they were the signs of his own weight and a sufficien.

Rommel's decorations and recognitions were instrumental in bolstering his reputation within the German military. They provided tangible evidence of his capabilities and the high regard in which he was held by his superiors. This recognition was crucial in establishing Rommel as a leader of exceptional talent and potential, setting the stage for his future rise to prominence., The awards he got stood proxy for his unparalleled authori. gness and his spectacul. leading to the accomplishment of miraculous testimony amidst the most difficult circumstances.

Besides the Pour le Mérite and the Iron Cross, Rommel was honored with other honors that were clear proof of his impressive performance. Those were various campaign medals and commendations that were issued to note his various contributions to the different theaters of war, as well as his consistent display of bravery and leadership. Every insignia one added to the lengthening list of awards were the ones marking Rommel's career and making him more popular as one of the most respected military leaders in Germany.

Rommel's recognition on parts beyond the battlefield. He often got praises from his superiors for his tactical acumen and his ability to inspire and lead his soldiers. General Friedrich von Below, one of Rommel's commanders, praised his extraordinary skills and observed his potential to become a commander in the future. Such recommendations were important both in his career growth and in getting Rommel's skills noticed and utilized in more and more important roles.

The honors and decorations Rommel received also had a great impact on his personal development as a leader. They implanted in him a strong sense of duty and a firm resolution to always be at the very top in his awards. Rommel's investing of himself into his great army and his mission were furthermore stamped out by the recognition he got, pushing him ever to excel in defense as well as offense.

In his command position, Rommel's decorated image was more crucial to his leadership style and his tactics during World War II. The knowledge and maturity he acquired during World War I, coupled with the appreciation of his accomplishments, stressed his way of thinking on race and his mastery of the entire battlefield when it was complex and the combat environment was dynamic. The awards were both his foundations and successes thanks to them he felt even more ready and assertive to oversee large-scale operations and make the most definitive decisions.

The legacy of Rommel's titles and distinctions goes beyond his personal accomplishments. They are a testimony to the natural talents of a great general, such as courage, novelty, flexibility, and a deep responsibility to duty. Achieving Rommel's medals is the result of his individual efforts, but it is also the end product of the higher doctrines of successful military leadership. The medals illustrate the point of strengthening devotion and the benefits it can bring to a leader's career, as well as the ability to exhilarate and lead people.

When we review the medals and rewards Rommel was presented with, it is seen that the medals were not only symbols of success. They were the sum of his time, talent, and think-tank, and played a very crucial role in the actualization of his different roles which made him a very respected and promising military leader in the 20th century. His acclaims had been indicative of his outstanding service and had been the chief architect of the history of military strategy and leadership. By his bravery and strategic thinking, Rommel was the one who set the bar high and in this way, the others registered his remarkable leadership and they have gone ahead to practice them in military commands to date.

The Genesis of a Military Legend: Rommel's Early Career

Since Rommel's young military service was for the most part, unique because he was a very disciplined efficient commander with very aggressive tactics very few men did not follow his path in history. Though, as a young man these learning years were crucial in shaping him into one of the ablest and most powerful generals of the 20th century. Through his first enlistment in the German Army to his commendable gunning during World War I, Rommel had presented an extraordinary demonstration of not only his solo leadership skills but also his strategic thinking which was the starting point for his future success.

Rommel's choice to fight in the military in 1910, at the age of 18, was just the beginning of the long journey that would reach its peak with him becoming an international figure. Promoted as a first lieutenant in the 124th Infantry Regiment, which was named the 6th Württemberg Infantry Regiment, Rommel had the chance to prove himself. His first duties were the most important in the process of training for the small-unit tactics, and leadership, which, however, were boring in comparison with the battles he fought later on. This was the time when he got some of the best experiences in his active military carrier and a deep understanding of infantry operations through his postings. It was in those years that Rommel first exhibited his traits as a leader with exceptional adeptness for using technology for his future accomplishments.

A changing event concerning Rommel's career happened when the World War I came to the stage in 1914. Situated on the Western Front, he was one of those who during the first days of the war got to know the reality of battle giving up the illusion of it as a heroic act always. Moreover, the new battlegrounds were against the training challenges he had learned but he became accustomed in no time. The events of those early battles brought the product of mobile warfare, mobility, flexibility, and maintaining decisive action. The poser of mobility, flexibility, and decisive rather than indecisive action in combat were exhibited by Rommel. Rommel's theatrical and otherwise theoretical behavior possibly set him apart from his colleagues and definitely marked him as one of the most distinguished among the.

Rommel's participation in the Battle of Caporetto in 1917 was among the most important episodes of his service in World War I. This battle, also known as the Twelfth Battle of the Isonzo, was a major achievement for the Central Powers against the Italian Army. Leading a small unit, Rommel adopted groundbreaking infiltration strategies, thus bypassing the heavily fortified enemy positions, and striking the rear and the flanks. His imaginative response to harsh conditions and exacting operations with precision are truly remarkable. The victory at Caporetto, where Rommel's group captured crucial points and took large numbers of prisoners with few losses, was that his tactical skills were recognized and that his star began to rise in the German Army.

Rommel's feat at Caporetto did not go unnoticed either. His courage and leadership were rewarded by several prestigious decorations, one of them being the Pour le Mérite, Germany's highest military honor at that time. This award was given to him for the excellent service he provided and the high esteem he had from his background. Besides the Pour le Mérite, Rommel received the Iron Cross First and Second Class, along with other awards. These distinctions did not only underline his personal successes but they also helped him further his career in the German military. Rommel's courage and art of war made him be respected and admired by his colleagues and leaders, which enabled the future of his rise to fame.

The medals and the other official honors Rommel was adorned by held a much larger significance than just being numismatic evidences of his victorious army life; each one of them was itself a clear affirmation of his outstanding revolutionary judgment and military leadership. These tokens that he received were a shield and proof of his power to command more complex and bigger battles. Rommel was a hero with medals who learned a lot from the past to directly influence his future leadership skills and successfully manage wars.

The courage, originality, and distinctive mettle of Rommel, which characterized the early stages of his military career, became his capital in his later accomplishments as a leader in the military. It was precisely his initial move into the military nearly the earliest jobs and the actual war trench experience in the outbreak of events in the World War I which had played the seminal role in crystallizing his tactical and leadership skills. The inner circle of the German army was more than interested to see Rommel perform like this at the famous Battle of Caporetto by demonstrating his absolute tactical brilliance and to some extent ensuring his future rising position as a fabulous soldier within the German army. The medals and awards he received added to his military power and made his future incursions during World War II possible. This part is specifically focused on Rommel's military origins and gives little-known details about the formative encounters that revolutionized his att-itude to warfare and leadership.

Rommel set off as a young lieutenant and ended up as a highly decorated and honored officer because of a series of turning points and accomplishments. All the steps were quite instrumental in bringing about his leadership and military strategy growth. His skills and abilities to innovate, adapt and lead well especially under the most challenging conditions were fully developed by the time he was serving as a lieutenant. The experiences and acknowledgment that followed concrete the groundwork for later victories and establish him as a legend in the military.

Rommel's initial journey became a permanent example of the key features that define as uplifted military leadership: valor, innovation, flexibility, and the devotion to obligation. His statements and acts during World War I not only displayed his zenithal tactical power but also were a preamble to the developments that came. The building of his first fame during these early years clothed the road to his reward with the nickname "Desert Fox" in World War II and in historical perspective had a lasting effect on the battlefield of the future.

Considering Rommel's early military journey, it is evident that his instruction, intelligence in exploring new ideas, and the courageous were part of his battlefield tactics as well as the style of management. They contributed incredibly to his training that he acquired at the beginning of his career as well as his practical knowledge and his intrepidness. The rise of Rommel from a recently graduated lieutenant to a renowned military chief brings out some of the eternal rules of style leadership such as passionate devotion to the cause, fearlessness, and creative thinking on the battlefield. Rommel, with his deeds and wins, laid the foundation for a class of the best that have since gone forward and have become the repository of the men and women who lead armed forces to this very day.

Chapter 3

Interwar Years

Navigating Challenges: Rommel's Post-WWI Military Career

The World War I was time of great problems and also of richest days for Erwin Rommel as just after the Tarding of Versailles that presented him with the difficulties of peacetime army duty in the Weimar Republic, he had already begun to learn the nature of military conflict in the era of mass consensus. The soldiers were demoralized by the severe provisions of the Treaty of Versailles that made the German army believed to be of no use, reducing the size and the possibility of developing new technology and taking advantage of new tactical methods. However, even this regulation stimulated Rommel's career in numerous ways that led to his promotion to higher ranks and to the mastery of the so-called swords complex, which is when the individual's qualities of primary collectivism, leadership, and militarism completion are balanced.

A treaty that has been imposed on a weak country like the Treaty of Versailles, which led to drastic cut of 100,000 troops, and that made impossible the development of tanks, and aircraft, is a serious blow to the German Army. This infantry replaced the Imperial German Army, which rather than he. Thus, the Reichswehr was charged with the responsibility to ensure the well-being of their fellows in the country and the production of the military arsenal within the bound of the agreement. The trial times were not able to stop Rommel from taking a front in the service office.

Rommel was not demobilized but joined the Reichswehr and, being the brainy officer with him, he was content to be promoted and tackle new challenges. This is the time when the main idea was his professional growth and the sharpening of his tactical and leadership skills. With these tasks, Rommel gradually got the necessary knowledge and skills of training and day-to-day handling of soldiers throwing the base for a bright military future.

"At one point, one of Rommel's assignments was as a company commander, and he had to use his leadership skills and tactical acumen he had in a practical way," became the early simple lyric. Guiding the infantry unit, that was a company with Rommel at its head, he made a special effort to strictly follow the requirements of the treaty. The capacity to be optimistic or forward-looking and keep the commitment to the basics, together with his approach to the matters of dry but efficient training, not only energised his troops, but also raised the level of knowledge so that they became better than before. This personal training had a very positive role in shaping his approach and the dissection of ill-defined interconnections in his leadership of military operations.

While Rommel was moving up the ranks of the army, he held several staff positions that gave him knowledge of military operations and strategy on a large scale. The role of these occupations composed of him to act at a higher level by formulating the plans of the different activities which have been, from the beginning to the end, a massive help in his strategic and organisational skills. Similarly, his problem-solving skills were mirrored in his staff positions, signifying his prestige as a "performance first" professional, as well as his ability to transform in accordance with the changes of the profession.

One of the great post-war aspects of the life of Rommel is his dedication to continuous learning and professional development. He had the ambition to know things not only in a military sense but also in the modern world along the lines of different fields. By the way, his practice of self-education was evident through his enrolment in different military courses and training programs, where he was able to teach and at the same time to learn advanced strategies. In this way, Rommel's professional development aspect could be characterized with a theoretical, practical duality wherein the new ideas he gets are very well integrated into his command style.

Despite the limitations of the Versailles Treaty, the German Army, however, managed to come up with new innovations and to adapt often in secret. Rommel was a very active member of the team in these projects. He not only participated but also was key to the development of new tactical maneuvers, and the improvement of training techniques that was soon to be used during World War II. His involvement in these illegal activities confirmed his commitment to rebel the standard military system and to try new combat tactics.

One of the main projects at that time was the "Hundred Thousand Man Army Concept". This program was to build a very excellent trained and very versatile military force under the Treaty limitations. Rommel was the first to come up with the idea of implementing this program. He was obsessed with focusing on the most strenuous and the most dynamic combat troops as well as the most adaptable battalion. His vital role was indicative of his thinking ahead and he was quite successful to introduce innovation within the limitations he had

After the war, however, Rommel had the opportunities to work with the new military instruments and concepts. Although his attempts to build tanks and aircraft were not allowed, Rommel himself further concentrated on these topics and endeavored to predict the outcomes of the issues may have on the warfare of the future. His initial actions where at the motorized infantry and the mechanized tactics. He believed that the flexibility and mobility of the warriors are the prime tools for triumph in the war. In the process, the principles of mobility and flexibility, which later on became his chief command style during the war, were synthesized.

Throughout the interwar years, Rommel was seen as a very good and thoughtful officer that was loved by almost everyone. His service in various jobs as a commander and staff officer, along with his commitment to professional development, strengthened his position within the Reichswehr. Rommel's ability to avoid the problems of peacetime service and to develop his knowledge of tactics and his skills of a leader was new and different, so he was recognized as a forward-thinking and efficient leader.

With the approach of the 1930s and the rise of the Nazi regime, Rommel's career experienced a quite important turn which consisted of the rearmament of the German army first. His links with the Nazi Party, particularly his relationship with Adolf Hitler, acted as a gate to high-status jobs and allowed him to try out his creative thinking in a bigger way. Although Rommel was not a member of the Nazi Party, his official connections with its chiefs were what helped him to grow professionally and to take the lead in the reorganisation and the modernisation of the German military.

Erwin Rommel's career after the First World War was an important one, in which he gained professionally, intellectually, and in knowledge of his field. Despite the terms placed on them by the Treaty of Versailles, Rommel's persistence, adaptability, and determination to be professionally excellent not only helped him to steer clear of the obstacles of the peace-time military but also contributed immensely to his future. His experiences during this time were significant in moulding his stance on leadership and warfare, and gave him the skills and knowledge required to turn into one of the best-known military leaders in the 20th century. By constantly making instructionss and his dedication to continuous learning and innovation, Rommel emerged from the interwar period as a formidable and forward-thinking officer, ready to take on the challenges of the next great conflict.

Anchored in Love: Rommel's Personal Life and Family

The interwar period was a time of lots of changes in the life of Erwin Rommel, it was not only his professional career but also his personal life that was transforming. This time was, above all else, one of progress and balance, nearly exclusively on account of the constant backing and love of his darling wife, Lucie Maria Mollin, whom he married in 1916. Their bond was such that Lucie Maria Mollin was an anchor to Erwin Rommel in those days. She was the only person who could give him a sense of home and rootedness at the time when the world was in chaos.

Lucie Maria Mollin was a key player on the ground, helping Rommel with her unwavering support and encouragement all through his profession. They were tied together by the wonderful relationship they had and the deep love they felt toward each other, and that was what kept it all together with the difficulties and the hills they had to walk. For her ballast, Lucie, moreover, played a consequential part in sharing hope and comforting Rommel, during the tightrope walk between personal success and relationship success.

They were both overjoyed to have their son Manfred, who was born in 1928. Manfred's arrival shocked the couple into silence. On its arrival, both of them, Rommel and Lucie seemed to have been given the family bond and got its strength further secured. Rommel's family made him feel better about things, had a strong core and they were definitely happy; these family moments were not as difficult to cope with as the strains that came with work. His wife and son's presence seemed to return him to peace and rejuvenation.

Despite his service in a military atmosphere, General Rommel was very much devoted to his family. He meticulous efforts to Lucie and Manfred were which contributed to a warm relationship in the family. This love for his family was revealed through the numerous letters to Lucie that he wrote while assigned to many different places. These letters show him as a man who had great love for his family, often telling them how much he missed them and the hopes for their future. By means of these letters, the human side of Rommel appears distinct from his military personality, showing their position as a loving husband and father.

Rommel's connection to his family was characterized by a very strong sense of duty and loyalty. He looked at his roles as a spouse and father very solemnly, who was aware of the significant role of emotional and practical support. Even though he was away most of the time because of his service, Rommel engaged consistently in the current affairs of Lucie and Manfred. His letters were usually packed full of detailed questions about their health, thus showing his overweening care of their joy and safety.

At this time, the family of Rommel became more influential in strong-temperedness of his character during the interwar period. Interwar Germany faced a host of social and economic challenges, as well as being under the heavy restrictions proposed in the Treaty of Versailles by the Allies. During the times when he encountered these difficulties the family support and the fact that he had a stable life were major contributors to the development of Rommel and the discovery of his personal strength.

Romalea was also much influenced by Lucie, The two supported each other in both their personal and professional lives. She always stood by her beloved one, gave him directions and guidelines, and cheered him when he was in doubt. However, it was Lucie's views and contributions that always made him think clearly and therefore enabled him to escape from mistakes in the future. The girl was always a factor for Ramel, who decided that certain principles make him act the way he does and that he should always remain depressed and lifted in his dreams.

Rommel's letters to Lucie on different assignments in the army, his letters to Lucie, they are a beautiful story of the general both as a person and a general. These letters contain so much love and pain, the person who has written them values his family or loves his family very much. In addition, the content of Rommel's letters often touches on and can represent the more personal side of him as he shares thoughts and feelings about the recent events, reflections on military strategy, and, of course, his dreams in life. Besides, Rommel has been known for his inward looking and also his being a family man who could balance his career and responsibilities.

Although Ramel loved his family and made it his top priority, Romantic implications are also evident in the way he led them. The fact that he was understanding of the need for emotional care and personal connections had an impact on how he treated his soldiers. Ramel is one of the many people who, with me, share the same perspectives. Due to his behavior that revealed affection for the men, he thus avoided many problems. His concern for the welfare of his soldiers just like his commitment to his family supported the ideals of perseverance, duty, and taking care of people for which he was known both personally and professionally.

The arrival of Manfred added another depth to Rommel's life, which served both to intensify his sense of connection with the world and his feeling of needing to care. As a father, Rommel was trying to make sure that his son got at least fleshly comfort and the loving environment. Participation in Manfred's education became one of the most exciting moments in his life. The most important source of wisdom and example for Manfred. He was the father who showed his son the way of integrity, the power of perseverance and just how fantastic the web of dedication, as well as all the other values, can be.

Rommel's family always showed that it was a fortress from which he got emotional fuel to go out in society and face whatever would come his way. The home constituted a safe place for Rommel where he could retreat if need be. Lucie and Manfred were the embodiment of love and they made Rommel safe and strong thus, able to resist all the threats that interwar brought his way. The family relationship acted like a big anchor that keeps him focused, both professionally and personally.

Fundamentally speaking, besides his professional career, Rommel's personal life and family were the fundamental drone of his well-being and success. The comfort zone induced by Lucie and Manfred helped him Shapture Sunder, low homelessness. The compassion he felt for his charges to his family combined with his job success was a man who considered personal responsibility and relation just as equally as his duty to the military. The love and backing of the family were vital in his character formation and the actions he undertook also in the battlefield.

Forging Tactical Prowess: Rommel's Interwar Military Education and Training

The period between the two world wars was the time of Rommel's growth as a soldier. Here he was demonstrating a deep devotion to increasing his military education and training in every way possible. The German military's innovation and adaptation in secret were despite the severest restrictions caused by the Treaty of Versailles, which placed national restrictions on the military come in the interwar period. These were also the times when the German military was forced to resort to other forms of development and innovation. He was a leading figure in this domain owing to his active participation in designing new war strategies and training that would eventually be used in the Second World War.

The Versailles Treaty was the first long-term entry of severe constraints on the scale and the quality of the German military, forcing it to come down to 100,000 troops and precluding it from making use of refined kinds of development. As much as they were cut back, the Germans had a hunger for finding legal means of evasion. To achieve this, they concentrated on the quality and adaptability of their men. Rommel's connection to these clandestine missions was proof of his dedication to professional high-caliber work. This he had displayed through his being an innovator despite the many restrictions he was subjected to.

One significant thing in Erwin Rommel's military education in the interwar years was his engagement in the founding and diffusion of infantry tactics. Rommel was both the teacher and the student in the various schools he was assigned to. This experience was critical in not only elevating his conception of a modern warfare system but also enabling him to guide the next wave of German officers using his personal insights. He did not teach as an authority figure, but instead, he disposed of the pose of an intellectual exchange and a platform for experimentation of tactics.

Rommel's method for teaching military was very special during this time. He was using a practical method that was flexible, initiative, and aggressively action-oriented. These maxims, that he had perfected in the First World War, were the fundamental words of his teaching doctrine. Rommel thought that by the means of his belief that the ability of mind was absolutely necessary for them to survive and win. The method of instruction saw this view confirmed with the use of realistic training scenarios and the officers were encouraged to strive to find their own solutions to tactical problems.

The undercover op of Germany's military improvements during the interwar years demanded a lot of originality and care that could be noticed by very few people. Rommel's decision how to go through the obstacles was the proof of the fact that he was a very resourceful man very much inclined to improve the abilities of the German army to the highest level. He took part in the secret military simulations and his ideas were the basis of the new doctrines containing the lessons of the Great War. The realization of these works was the period during which the German military got ready for the sacking of the Versailles Treaty regulations and the re-equipment that would go with it.

The book called "Infiltration Has always been the way" (Infanterie greift an) was published in 1937 that marked the history of Rommel's writing and publication of the book was in 1937 and this moment defined his interwar career in a significant manner. This book was a detailed account of Rommel's experiences during World War I, providing practical insights into infantry tactics and battlefield leadership. "Infantry Attacks" was the book which was regarded as the fundamental learning material in the field of military education, it was also highly appreciated for its clear and vivid descriptions of war scenes and its emphasis on the topics being flexible and functioning. Military Romans' reputation as a military thinker and the changes in the Army's tactics in the years preceding World War II could not be discussed without including this book publication.

"Infantry Attacks" displayed Rommel's conviction that adaptability is major in the changing dynamics of a battle. He stressed the fact that the officers should lead from the front and be quick decision-makers and that they should exploit chances and act accordingly without delay. A different approach than the one steered by more rigid and hierarchical structures, which were the reflections of the pre-war doctrines. Rommel's approach to decentralized command and gave more power to junior officers was groundbreaking and was a strong point of German tactics during World War II.

Rommel as an instructor gained a lot of experiences that were vital in shaping the base of his leadership and strategic management. Telling of this story, Rommel, a military instructor, explained that the process of instructing military officers in the latest military strategies was a two-way process that allowed him to better his own strategic planning in a continuously evolving military landscape and get knowledge of cutting-edge military theory. His contact with the young officers also gave him new perspectives and suggestions, which, in turn, created an atmosphere where mutual learning and growth can be nurtured. Such talks through experience and wisdom were of prime importance to keep Rommel's plans effective and in popular sentiment.

Similarly, the interwar years had been utilized by Rommel in seekers of ongoing professional development. He had taken part in both military courses and programs, teaching some of them, while also attending as a student. They got the idea of different disciplines; from advanced infantry tactics to the rising areas of mechanized and armored warfare. Rommel had a reflex dedication to life-long learning being proclaimed through the compilation of qualitative evidence supporting the assertion that Rommel's ingenuity was continuously influenced by his hunger for knowledge, allowing him to be the first of several commanders to develop and employ ground-breaking new technologies in his units.

Rommel, who was responsible for creating and developing the military capacities of Germany in the time between the two world wars, did not stop at educational facilities and training their personnel. He was also a participant in the secret rearmament programs that were the rock bottom for the recovery of the German army as a military power. These activities included the alleged attraction of the tanks, planes, and other high-tech weapons secretly or via foreign countries. His contribution and his revelation in this field willingness should be remarked and signature note of his, of his professional and social faculty modulation through the subtle and increasingly perilous mazes of hidden military activities.

The period from the end of the World War I to the beginning of World War II can be seen as Germany's greatest as a nation.

Along with other countries, where they developed new strategies and planned new technologies, the period from the end of the World War I to the beginning of World War II saw the cessation of Germany's ban on trade but a continuous procession of this hegemonic German nation, the game of the treaties, the promises all done to be broken and the life with the set rules and re-contextualized theoretical underpinnings. Focusing on Rommel, his talent in modernizing the well-known battlefield monuments and incorporation of kindred theories into his nuclei that immortalized him as the best of many who ever served the purpose of the German military.

The pre-war period was a time when Erwin Rommel had a remarkable professional development. He conveyed the newer art of learning and the distinct features of his innovative imagination like the pride of place it bears with military training and development, further qualified in his role in the furtive rearmament of Germany. The trials of his ambitions led to an ever-deepening process of knowledge that allowed both Rommel and other professionals to absorb creative concepts at places where circumscribed capacities modified the common linguistic formative expression.

Tactical Mastery: Rommel's 'Infantry Attacks'

A period before World War II was crucial in the life of Erwin Rommel, characterized by its peak: his work "Infantry Attacks" (Infanterie greift an.) influenced the world of literature by turning into the best reference book. In 1937, Rommel was presenting his arguments when the book, which was the truest account of what he had been through during the First World War, was published. It may certainly be stated that the book tops the rest for it offers very deep insights into tactical decision-making, the masterstroke of Rommel's approach to combat.

"Infantry Attacks" appears to be an outstanding choice for franchise. It is not a mere militia but a book that Bonaparte had designed to transmit the training Rommel had received at first hand. The account is so designed that it makes an in-depth record that deals with the different fights and interprets the difficulties achieved and the strategies applied to carry out the fighting successfully. Through such detailed narration, Rommel highlights the cutting-edge features of modern warfare, highlighting the issues of the urgency of taking initiative, being flexible, and acting bravely, principles that he would follow during his command in the second World War.

According to "Infantry Attacks," it is obvious that Rommel gives priority to the initiative. His study is highlighted by many examples where officers used to make quick decisions and acted independently and forcefully, a necessary pre-condition of battles in the modern world. Rommel was of the opinion that the background would get complicated rapidly and the persons at the helm should be smart in their decision to continue. The initiative strategy is stressed upon in some instances that you can even believe that just rationalizing and being bold can get them there even despite their disadvantaged situation.

Another key concept revealed in this account is flexibility. The experiences that Rommel had in the First World War were the ones that gave him a real understanding of adaptability in battles. The ever-changing form of the battlefield made rigid plans lose their strength when the pressure came and, therefore, improvising to new situations became a matter of life and death and success. Diverse examples in Rommel's stories point to these situations and show that he was extremely flexible and responsive not just to things that happened, but those also that were unforeseen. His agility was, therefore, greatly appreciated and expected in the situation of scantness of time, and he was able to respond adequately to the German enemy's actions. What we see now is how the same flexibility would be characteristic of his leadership in the Second World War thus he used it as a means of grabbing the opportunities that his enemies were giving and also of acting effectively on their movements.

The other side of evolution, that is aggressiveness, can be identified through pushing back the enemy in order for the them to use their own last target. Noticing the value of this quality in the written text about war, the great German military leader Rommel is found to be the one who adhered to this principle all the time. His eyewitness in the first place thought of the necessity of keeping the initiative all the time, and for this reason, he made use of the ideas of speed and surprise to obstruct and overpower the adversary. According to him, a proactive manner was the most vital thing in the initiative so that it is maintained and the narrative seems to agree with his thoughts, arguing over project leaders to grab the moment and put more weight on the "real" side. Thus this very mindset of hitting hard was the one that went in to become a central pivot to Rommel's later campaigns in the Second World War, where his bold tactics and unceasing attacks landed him the short name of the "Desert Fox".

"Infantry Attacks" not only led Rommel to make a personal achievement but also contributed to military education largely. The straightforward advice and thorough examination made it an inevitable resource for military officers and strategists. It then came to be acknowledged in military academies and hence became a major player in shaping the tactical doctrines of the German Army in the years prior to World War II. Thus Rommel did really lay the groundwork by providing his suggestions on small-unit tactics, maximization of the hand of command while under fire and the fusion of infantry with other arms of service with reference to the new developing strategies and doctrines.

"Infantry Attacks" is a reflection of Rommel's commitment to the fluid dynamics of battles. His experience by pointing out several fight will hold the views that unanticipated barriers and the environment's swapping of a hostile nature compel the use of multiple approaches, are also shown. The book consistently reiterates Rommel's talent to shift and transform plans in a flexible way and to find the solution in the very stress of the concept of the warfare environment changing in virtually real-time. This adaptability, a lesson learned by him in the crucible of war, was an essential message that Rommel tried to communicate to his readers.

The penetration of the book into other spheres, including the outside Germany, is a result of the appreciation of this piece of literature among different military experts. "Infantry Attacks" was made into several languages and also published in various battle write-ups of officers across the globe, emphasizing its appeal to humans and non-humans as well as the standing of its lessons as timeless. The concepts the author promoted can be related to modern military leaders who were confounded with the confusion of war. The book's emphasized instance studies and direct, clear explanations enabled the axes to the broad public.

"Infantry Attacks" is unique among others for its extraordinary and arresting style of writing. Rommel brings the real-life situations of the war battle into a clear and unambiguous way which makes the book to be informative and captivating. He tells the story in a way that makes one feel like the battle is going on, and thus one senses, the hardness and the satisfaction of soldiers in the battle lines. This captivating way of expressing himself is more than just making someone understand the book. More importantly, it guarantees its long-term status as a military literature dignitary.

Through his work of "Infantry Attacks" Rommel's career can be said to have been shaped to a very large extent. The volume has reinforced his reputation as a military theoretician and pioneer, thus winning him approval and respect not only within the German army but also in the wider world. It was his tactical mastermind and the way how he could extract the most practical lessons from his experiments that were exhibited, thus underlining his identity as a thinker who put into practice both intellectual ardor and technical expertise. This esteem helped him to get positions and to rise above everything else later during World War II.

Concisely put, "Infantry Attacks" is a foundational piece which encapsulates the core of Rommel's tactical outlook and his outlook towards fighting. Being an initiative, flexible, and aggressive as well as being practical and vividly explaining the facts and the varieties of the treatments, made the book an important focal point for the military to learn. The book's influence on military doctrines, and its role in solidifying Rommel's status as a military thinker, underscores its lasting relevance. "Infantry Attacks" is a proof of Rommel's strategic skills and his capability of turning his battlefield stories into evergreen lessons for the next periods of military leaders.

Ascending the Ranks: Rommel's Promotions and Key Assignments

To be recognized as one of the best soldiers in history, Erwin Rommel ran the interwar period quite astoundingly. The whole period was a step by step climb up into a new entity, starting as a member of the Reichswehr and turning later on into the formidable Wehrmacht, the conductor armed forces of Nazi Germany. In every promotion, he took on new responsibilities which gave him an opportunity to provide creative and brilliant answers both through his talented leadership and his strategical thinking in the military.

Rommel's assignment and he was in command of a group were brilliant in those days. As the commander of this unit he was able to put his tactical knowledge and leadership style into practice while he was the leader of a company of infantrymen. In the opinion of subordinates, Rommel was not a typical bureaucratic leader as his characteristic leadership approach was leading by example, for example, he got into the field, attended the activities that developed the abilities of the forces and showed the same physical and mental stability, his soldiers had to have. As a result, he was loved and received the dedication from his subordinates who also noticed the close fraternity created from his wise and sensible style of leadership. The magic he presented was not only in his ability to coach but also in his unselfish attitudes towards teammates thus he was the best player. A great way of proving that Rommel was a fantastic leader was his strong effectiveness when it comes to leading his troops and the great example he set of being an effective leader through his action of leading by example.

When Rommel's reputation for the reason that he is known for his well-thought-out approach to leadership and his comprehension grew, he was then the youngest of the battalion's generative commanders. Notably, he gained outstanding interpersonal and social integration skills in this aspect. As one of the crew commanders, he gave a seat belt demonstration to his company. His knowing of military tactics and materials was deepened in this stage of his duty. This evidently was a result of the lack of detail in his organization and the abilities of adaptation to the circumstances he was, serving the military at the time and hence these positions were a great reflection of his role as a detailed planner and as an adaptive service person.

The late 1930s became the turning point in Rommel's career that put him in control of the ultimate The Theresian Military Academy Wiener Neustadt, Austria, became, commanding officer. The distinguished post was a sign of Rommel's prominence and popularity in the German army. As commandant, Rommel had the main responsibility of supervising the training and development of future officers. This position gave him the opportunity to be the leader of the next batch of military leaders who had learned the teachings he had found and the things that he wrote throughtout his own experiences.

Rommel in the military school tried to modernise and renovate the lessons in the curriculum and introduce modern tactical doctrines. Building on his successful war years and the interwar period, he built training programs that prioritised the initiative, flexibility, and aggressive action—these are the principles that he put down in his "Infantry Attacks" book. The widespread of Rommel's innovation at the academy is sufficient, in that he taught the importance of flexibility in the flow of a battle and the importance of taking the necessary speedy and short decisions that come with it. The field of the battlefield education/retraining and revitalization of Romöll's implemented plans were crucial in the German officer corps getting ready for the challenges of World War II.

His way through the ranks was as a result of his connections to the Nazi Party, especially his connection to Adolf Hitler. Due to Rommel's military genius and people skills - gives plusses, he was chosen to interact with Hitler's trusted agents. Though he was not a member per se, his close professional relationship with the Nazi leaders meant he found ways of getting positions and groups that were able to implement his highbrow ideas on a larger scale. It should be obvious that Hitler so much counted himself lucky to get Rommel amidst such aide from the first years of World War Two to the point where he recommended the obvious torch-bearer the leader of major military operations.

Rommel, through his wartime career, had a memorable and important job of the successful invasion of Poland in 1993. The courageous Rommel, commander of the Führerbegleitbrigade, which is Hitler's personal escort brigade, was able to perform really well. Besides being a good soldier, Rommel's proximity to Hitler enabled him to further express his talent and creativity in tactical moves. His actions on the front lines in Poland showed everyone that he was a commander with great potential and boldness. Trusting him even more, Hitler had given him more and more power and responsibility.

The story of Rommel's life was such that he was promoted to the highest leadership position in the 7th Panzer Division when the French Invasion happened in 1940. Moreover, this mission was a decisive moment in his military path, as he was efficient in the leadership of his troops, quickly attacking his enemy as a result of his braveness, and his nickname was "the Ghost Division" because of the fast and unpredictable movement of the company. Rommel's management in the French campaign showed that he was capable of implementing the warfare strategies with lightning speed and surprise attacks that p whispered out from the German ranks.

Taking over the French campaign was a great place to start for Rommel, but his time in North Africa was even better, as he gained profound admiration that was shown through his attachment to the nickname "Desert Fox." His actions in North Africa marked his ascendancy over all others in the Strategic domain due to his strategic intelligence and his ability to adjust to the desert environment. His actions in the North African campaign demonstrated his skills to motivate his soldiers and outsmart his enemies, becoming not only a respected but also a feared leader.

Rommel was known throughout his career for his promotions and his key assignments; a demonstration that he possessed a magnificent lead, and his tactics were of a newer kind. Besides e-learning and the professional development, hands-on approach of management, he was able to perform well in all roles through his continuous learning. His innovations, not only on the field, also had an impact on the army's diversity in skills, how it reasoned, and decision-making.

As the result of his ability to motivate and guide his troops, the tactic of his tactical genius and his commitment to professional excellence, Rommel's promotions through the ranks of the Reichswehr as well as the Wehrmacht are to be admired. His path was a direct reflection of the unyielding devotion and fidelity he had to his country and how he saw the value of the adaptability and innovation in showing of military strategy. Rommel, as a military leader, is remembered for his fantastic job of maneuvering the times through his leadership which was marked by his vision and strategic quick-mindedness.

Crafting a Legend: Rommel's Formative Interwar Years

The interwar years were an extremely important time for Rommel, and so it was one of the strongest aspects of his military career. His time was marked with growth on both his professional and personal levels and he was able to develop intellectually as well. This period was the one that came after the terrible experiences of the First World War. It was for this reason that Rommel developed his right to the real leadership, strategic thinking, and setting the bases of the future success that would enter Europe in the role of the most talented general of World War II.

Erwin Rommel had to survive the increased confusion which his profession produced on receiving the orders from Germany's military operations after the end of the World War I. The Versailles Treaty was the document that was to be observed and that had limited the German military buildup over the making of severe restrictions on the Germans who had been strictly limited by the artwork of much of the country. To the left of it all, however, Rommel insisted on his sticking to the highest excellence of his profession in his work. It was the Reichswehr who took his name among the soldiers, he was given tasks which he not only accomplished well but proved his mastery of these commandments and staffing techniques. He was clearly a powerful figure in the new army development though all those who would invoke his name. The post-war activities which he faced during the Sudan crisis were very significant in terms of his now clear understanding of modern warfare and its leadership essentials.

It was during his post-World War I period that considered him qualified enough to provide him with different learning experiences such as junior staff and tactical management of his unit. These facilities, which brought you the knowledge of what was to be done and how soldiers should be led and governed, gave him the practical skills that he needed to practice after the army. Even his direct involvement with men was the infusion that brought him the required level of respect and loyalty from his subordinates. Through his pathos (the emotional appeal), he lived among the dead that made everyone believe in him and move on with courage even in the toughest battles. Rommel's incredible ability to excite and encourage hep to soldiers was evident in his natural-born leader skills and his sagacious communication. In fact, the Great Man behind those brave army soldiers had outstanding skills in understanding both the technological part of the war and the psychological one that pushed his men forward.

Surely one of the most vital aspects of the success of Rommel was the fact that he was able to keep his personal life unshaken throughout the years. His union with Lucie Maria Mollin in 1916 and their son Manfred's arrival in 1928 helped Rommel find peace and stability. Despite the demands of his military career, Rommel maintained a close relationship with his family, often expressing his desire to be with them and his hopes for their future in letters to Lucie. This intact family environment gave Rommel the psychological support he required to concentrate on his job and to continue his intellectual growth.

During the interwar years, one of the ingredients that contributed to Rommel's intellectual development was his execution of the military education process through his book, "Infantry Attacks" (Infanterie greift an). In 1937, this pioneering work acknowledged

Rommel's experiences in World War I which are responsible for producing the highly intellectual article that cuts into his mental processes of wars and battles which are his forte. "Infantry Attacks" has not only given birth to a whole new genre of military educational books but it is, in fact, the only one in the world, that detailed practical advice and exciting descriptions of the scenario among which one has to move in battle. The manual showed that Rommel was very concerned about taking charge, being flexible, and being aggressive actions when it was required thus emphasizing his command style during the Second World War.

"Infantry Attacks" had reached such a high level that led to the innovation of military theory in Germany. Rommel's creativity and thorough quantitative analyses formed the base for the new tactics and strategies that were later executed highly in World War II. The concepts of adapting to the mobility of warfare and the significance of concise, momentous undertakings were well-received by the military staff, both within Germany and around the world. The "Infantry Attacks" not only set the foundation for the conventions and doctrines to be used in the future but also became the source of influential innovation in relation to the German Army just before the war.

Rommel's professional development during the period between the two world wars was characterized by several rewardings and significant responsibilities that would help him demonstrate a greater output of his leadership ability. This was a career-defining event for Rommel; he became commandant of the Theresian Military Academy in Wiener Neustadt, Austria. This teaching post conferred him Rommel with the power of conditioning and knowledge of future officers, thus ensuring his position in the German army was secured. His time at the academy was highlighted by his efforts to modernise the syllabus and add his firsthand lessons with the objective of better preparing the next group of military officers for future challenges.

Rommel also capitalized on his ties with the Nazi Party which made his progress in the military smoother, particularly his relationship with Adolf Hitler. Rommel's blowing-away skills and glowing personality made a big impression on Hitler, who then chose him for high-profile jobs. Although Rommel was not a Nazi, he was still able to take advantage of the connections with Party leaders by using them to further his career and to apply his unconventional ideas to more sectors of the military. The link between Rommel and the Nazi elite was not only a turning point in the assignments he received there but it also opened the door to his involvement in military planning at senior levels.

The peacetime years were not only the preparatory years for Rommel but also his period of strongest influence and activity. The culmination of his efforts in personal development, the revolutionary changes he achieved in the field of military education, and his long history of success in various positions set the stage for more to come. Rommel acquired so much experience and knowledge during his time that it actually changed the direction of his war strategies, especially in terms of the military leadership dimension of the World War II.

Rommel's between-war years were marked by a non-stop hunt for the best and an unshakable commitment to unceasing improvement. His gift of being able to mold his conduct to unpredictable times, his concentration on the very workable, and practicalally also effective solutions, as well as his profound understanding of the very principles of leadership and war, took him out to the heads of military geniuses. The characteristics, that had been developed on the pre-war time period, later would lead to his world-renowned reputation as the "Desert Fox," a commander whose strategic wisdom and tactical inventiveness would probably be a new point in the history of military science.

The most important thing that the time of inter-war made to Erwin Rommel was that it became a crucial time period in his life. The years in between served as a platform for him to be able to acquire the necessary skills as a leader and get the essential practical knowledge and at the end put him in a position, of the most prominent figures in military education. His personal life's tranquility along with his family's encouragement not only alleviated the burdensome side but also aroused his concentration on his professional responsibilities and intellectual development. These years of career growth, personal stability, and intellectual development marked the beginning of Rommel's successful career and at the same time assured his place as one of the famous military personalities in the 20th century.

Chapter 4

Rise to Prominence

Early World War II Service - Rommel's Role in the Invasion of Poland

Erwin Rommel's ever-growing power in the military world commenced with his very first service in the World War II. As Germany's invaded Poland in September 1939, Rommel was nominated to command the Führerbegleitbrigade, which was the personal escort of Hitler. This very important role gave to Rommel a chance to be near Hitler, thus to show that his leadership skills were high and that he had the tactical expertise. The invasion of Poland was a crucial check for the German army that showed the beginnings of the blitzkrieg, which became the main tactics to win the war in the coming years that will define German strategy.

The Führerbegleitbrigade mission was to accomplish two tasks that are to secure Hitler and participate in the most important battles. This new mission was also another chance for Rommel to demonstrate his ability to carry out a critical operation on a big scale. The Polish campaign was carried out swiftly and effectively involving fierce assaults, in order to quickly cripple the enemy. Rommel's soldier squad also played a very crucial part in the campaign, thus backing the tough blitzkrieg strategy.

In the Polish invasion, the Führerbegleitbrigade of Rommel had the duty of securing Hitler as he moved up to the front line to keep the observation and direction of operations. This post gave Rommel a close look at the decision-making process of the Führer and the priorities in strategies. The nearness to Hitler also meant that Rommel's actions were watched very closely thus giving him a chance for both improving and being a challenge too. His speed in deploying the forces, his ability to control the soldiers well even under the sky falling down, and his responsive nature to the ever-changing battlefield were the key reasons of his triumph.

Rommel's interpretive ability is clear from the way he ran his brigade during the campaign. He stressed speed, surprise, and decisive action saying they were the most critical of the blitzkrieg doctrine. Rommel's skill in managing maneuvers to take advantage of weak points in the Polish defenses showed his knowledge of the demand of modern warfare. His lead-through-the example style, which is his way of gaining direct handling and leading from the front, developed in the soldiers a strong feeling of confidence and loyalty.

One interesting feature of Rommel's leadership through the Polish campaign was the ability to keep high discipline levels and lift the morale of his men. The blitzkrieg's tight tempo demanded more than just obedient soldiers who followed orders and responded to new directions and battlefield conditions as stated by the rapidly changing orders on the battlefields. Rommel's ability in evoking the sense of purpose and inclusiveness among his brigade was the support that they needed for their efficient performance. His command turned the unit into a single acting team and let a strong belonging feeling to grow, which helped the soldiers to be in the heat of the battle.

The steps which Rommel took during the Polish invasion did not go unnoticed. His capacity to produce swift and precise results won him praise from the highest-ranking officers in the Nazi Party, and even from Hitler. This endorsement was a key element in Rommel being quickly relocated and promoted through the hierarchical structure of the military. Hitler's admiration for Rommel's tactical brilliance, and his charismatic style of leading, were important parts of Rommel's inclusion in the planning for future high-profile commands.

The victory of the German attack in Poland obviously proved the effectiveness of blitzkrieg tactics, and Rommel's contribution to the whole struggle was a quite considerable part of this victory.

During the preliminary stages, the lightning war tactic had not only exceeded the expectations of the Polish army but also had revealed the military potential of Germany to the rest of the world. His participation in this group endowed him with the experience and acquaintance which then served as the grounds for people to recognize him as a commander coping with logistical and strategic issues in a new way such that he solved these issues in novel ways.

The genius of Rommel in the Polish campaign was the quality of his mind and work. The flexibility that he possessed in sharing the tasks of defending Hitler and participating in the conflict was the element of his capacity as a military leader. Rommel's ability to satisfactorily deal with the dynamics of the battlefield and to consistently focus on quick and proper actions were two most important aspects of his achievement. These traits became his leading features as he was an innovator in his future leadership models.

The contribution made by Rommel in Poland in terms of the approval he gained there served as the stepping stone for him to climb the ladder of success in his military career. The original way of fighting and skills of leadership so impressed Hitler and other top Nazi party officials that he was as a result of that period made to be a vital in more powerful positions. His triumph in Poland was a decisive moment in making him one of the top military leaders in Germany.

The blitz of Poland signified the start of World War-II and the emergence of Erwin Rommel being a major player in the German military. In the military exercise, the general had thus proved that besides his developing original methods of being a tactician, he was also very inspiring to his fellow fighters and even to his immediate bosses. The encounters and teachings in the events of war were petite, but they played a major role in his career as a warrior and the development of his timeless "De

Rommel's contribution to World War II was not just in the usual way. In Poland, he helped in carrying out a blitzkrieg, a lightning warfare strategy. This gave him the platform not only to show himself as a daring tactician but also as a commander in front of the audience. The greatness of his accomplishments is seen by the fact that he was promoted to the standing of the generals very quickly. In Poland, one can see that the blitzkrieg was indeed a reality and that Rommel's role was simply an example of his innovative approach and the wide use of his strategic knowledge. Through this time, Rommel's dedication to discipline continuously expanded, so, he could enjoy an increase of proficiency and mastery of modern warfare strategies. The time of his this was a not just professional growth of becoming an officer, but it was also a tested period of letting the oldest of the military tactics to get modernized.

Rommel's Campaign in France

After conquering Poland, Erwin Rommel was named as a key person in the broader German military action in France, which began in May 1940. The main aim of this operation was to get a fast victory in taking out the French and the Allied forces using blitzkrieg. It was known as blitzkrieg tactics, which were the quick, concentrated strikes meant to crush the enemy, that was employed in this campaign. Rommel's tactical abilities and leadership were clear in this operation where he was the commander of the 7th Panzer Division.

The struggle in France was the main part of the experiment in which the Germans checked their blitzkrieg strategy which was already established by their victory in Poland. The 7th Panzer Division, to which Rommel was assigned, took the lead in the introduction of the innovation. The major job of the division was to go deeper into the territory of the opponent, which was also identified as one of the means of troubling the enemy forces. Rommel's display of these abilities to reach the goals was characterized by an extraordinary rate of speed as well as accuracy which won him very many kudos and solidified his image as one of the strong military men in Germany.

FRANCE OCCUPIED BY AXIS POWERS
1940-1944

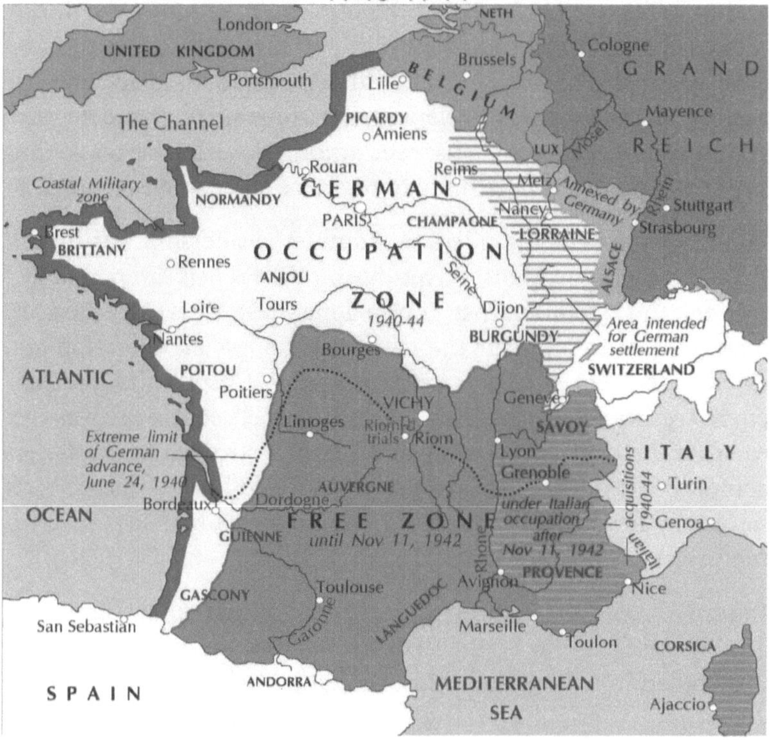

Rommel's approach during the French campaign was tied to the elements of quickness, unexpectedness, and the power of conclusions. He was able to design the blitzkrieg principles of its execution through fast speed manoeuvres with accuracy, going to the enemy territory and destroying their defenses. His quick adaptation to the changing front conditions and stubborn and uninterrupted activities on the sake of victory created great achievements for the German armed forces. Rommel's brilliant divisional advancement, along with the fast rate of groundbreaking, enabled Rommel to win the acclaim of many people and finally, he had been one of the strongest military leaders in Germany.

The skill of war tactics that Rommel owned was the way he directed his division during the campaign. He stressed the ideas of speed and mobility in the support of the movement of his units. Hence, he was able to move and strike fast. The method let Rommel can always surprise his enemy from different angles of attack and use their weak points in their defences. His use of surprise and decisive action caused chaos and disorder among the Allied troops, thus kept them from the possibility to organize an effective response.

The most important incident in Rommel's leadership was indeed the crossing of the Meuse River during the French campaign. It is through this operation that Rommel manifested his extraordinary management to integrate the parts of a completed operation and to execute them with the most precision. Despite the intensive enemy resistance, the division under Rommel's command was able to cross the river successfully and set up a stronghold. Rommel's achievement demonstrated that he possessed the strategic view necessary for a successful operation and was a true leader to his men even in difficult times.

Rommel's way of leading was defined by his direct approach and his readiness to be the first in the fight. Rommel commonly distributed himself in the midst of the fighting, sketching out the course of actions depending on the actual development of the battle-front. This method not only helped Rommel to know the real condition on the ground but besides that he succeeded in his troops, who were elevated by his realizing and exemplifying leadership. Rommel's ability to keep a high fighting spirit among his men and the squad-maintenance through even hard combat that proved to be his excellent leadership skills.

We all wonder how a superior thaniman could create miracles, not just by the help of his own unit members, but also by the enemy. The enemy was left in awe and panic due to the division's Domination of both, sudden disappearances and quick execution of the plan, and It seemed like a Ghost Division had Accomplished them. His stand that the unit should always have one move ahead of the enemy, and no panic, ALL WHOLE Stood for the initiation he showed by his leadership.

Rommel deserves to win the era of Mexico, however, not only because of his techniques but also for his talent to be top-notch and resourceful. He comprehended the value of coordination and his solution was traiting help from three different locations: infantry, armor, and air. Thus, the successful blending of these aspects led to the highest competition of Rommel's style of war that was for sure ending the end in his favor; the statement of so is named as the Tree of Life since the content made is still very much a part of the original version.

The benefits of Rommel's conduct during the campaign of France were not just local they could be seen in the overall project war. His application was able to come up with changes in strategy and tactics that brought understanding and embraced the new method. That way his blitzkrieg of the French is an excellent demonstration of the new type of war and that could be an outstanding suggestion for the operations of the future. Such a large number of people agreed on Rommel's performance that he was both honored and highly admired by his partners as well as his chiefs. Thou, The lessons thoroughly learned came only after the accomplishments of the commitments allowing Rommel to later use some of them in the different wars. Lay theard down his name as the ace in the whole deck of all generals.

The episode in France was one of the turning points in life and career of Rommel due to his command of Das, Dorf. The easiness with which Rommel was able to change his maneuvers and his ability to prompt the soldiers make the pointless commander be seen as an extraordinary leader working both with the pen and the sword. The truth on the one side and the thriving in the other gave Rommel their instruments because with the former and the latter a man is a predator thus the content of this statement was not changed, but one was only added and is the Tree of Life as well as the original one.

The unstoppable climb of Rommel in the Italian front during WW2 was accompanied by his application of the principle of the blitzkrieg, his style of leading by example, and his innovativeness in his tactical decisions. The performance of the "Ghost Division" in the first of the French campaign vividly portrayed his skill in using modern warfare and as well as a propeller for his future accomplishments. See to Rommel's biography would bring the most basic of his charisma and military capabilities that he would hold on for the rest of his life and be the only person in military history to do so.

Commanding the 7th Panzer Division (Ghost Division): Mastering Blitzkrieg

Erwin Rommel was the one who took command of the 7th Panzer Division during the French campaign in 1940. This was the pivotal period when he had to prove his military abilities, thus, becoming one of the most innovative and efficient military leaders in Germany. His leadership style was the most remarkable and the very one that got his division, the so-called "Ghost Division," known everywhere it went for executing Rommel's blitzkrieg tactics and his dynamic style of command. During the time Rommel took over the command post, the 7th Panzer Division completed series of rapid moves causing the enemy personnel to be bewildered and consequently leaving them unable to effectively defend themselves.

Rommel stood mainly as a direct, hands-on approach to his leadership is the main trait that set him apart from other commanders. He was recurrently the one in the frontline and he personally inspected tasks and made fast decisions based on the real situation at present on the battlefield. The notable proximity to the site did not prevent Rommel from forming a correct view of circumstances and from acting promptly when the conditions altered. The presence of Rommel near frontlines also kept the troops in high spirits - they were inspired by him as the main factor that motivated R...marine and as the uninterrupted commitment of Rommel, the leader of them. Rommel's relentless commitment to the moral and unity of the unit, though it was very hard because of the battle, was proof of his excellent leadership abilities.

The remarkable thing the 7th Panzer Division achieved goes mostly to Rommel's mastery of blitzkrieg tactics. The blitzkrieg strategy that Roman used, being rapid, attacking enemies in a concentrated way then overcoming and defeating them was best portrayed to be the next command of his offensive and adjustable command style. Through the use of mobility and firepower, he ensured his division¿s strikes were so quick they disrupted the adversaries¿ plans and, thus, opened up the possibility for further progress. His combination of arms, that included infantry, armor, and air support, was the force to be reckoned with in the sense that it had the highest level of influence on his assaults.

At the time of campaign in France, the 7th Panzer Division won several prominent victories that brought to light Rommel's tactical genius. One of these was their rapid crossing of the Meuse River. Besides the great resistance of French force, Rommel's unit managed to flood and found his army on the other side. This task has shown the capabilities of the coordination of the division and execution of complex movements with high accuracy, the abilities of the commander who carried out the operation. Besides the usual use of the scout units to gather real-time information and his desire to take the calculated risk that others had would not being a brute force was again the key to his operations.

One of the most notable accomplishments was the quick progress of the division through the Ardennes forest, an operation which is a perfect proof that Rommel was a great leader who is not hindered by natural barriers. The abrupt and steep terrain of the Ardennes was taken as impassable by many of the war strategists. But, the employment of that forest as the shortest way and advancing powerfully were the reasons which decided in Rommel's favor. Furthermore, his hitting them first with sexy moves made not only German soldiers call his division "Ghost Division" but also their enemies. The ability of the division to quickly launch a strike and withdraw even before the enemy could organize a scounteroffensive was what caused the feeling of dread and uncertainty towards them that the enemy forces had.

Rommel's conduct during this time was mainly characterized by his constant search for the lead. He was in no doubt aware of the significance of the lifeblood and probably disorienting his opponent through such motion. This was why he was successful all the time in making sure that his division always lead the opponents a step ahead of. For the reputation of the division on speeding and surprising the enemy except the adversary being still in shocked state, and the batteries aside there. Obviously, the last one is the biggest one because the enemy is actually being kept in a state of latent fear and getting rid of their initial shock.

The success of the 7th Panzer Division under Rommel's command carried out a significant part in the general German strategy. His accomplishment in the usage of the rush tactics exposed others to how this new form of warfare would work and as a result, also laid the ground for future operations. Rommel's struggles were largely noticed during his time, thus, gaining him many promotions and acknowledgment from both his superiors and peers. His tactical and leadership style were worthwhile topics and people began to study and even praise about the German military and of the whole world, actually.

Rommel's capacity to modify his military tactics according to the changing conditions of the battlefield is an essential ingredient of his triumph. He had a deep understanding of the fact that flexibility in combat is important thus he was able to adjust his original plans whenever the situation was changing. It was this characteristic that would lead him to dare and be an unbeatable adversary. His successful campaign in France showed the effectiveness of blitzkrieg tactics and proved the value of innovative thinking in military strategy.

The actual events that occurred in France and Rommel's command in the 7th Panzer Division were of the most fundamental importance in proving him to be one of Germany's most gifted and out-of-box military leaders. Rommel was convinced to change his game plan, learn to conduct quick and efficient moves and which was his tactic to motivate his soldiers made him a distinctive and exceedingly skilled and visionary leader. The strategies Rommel used in other parts of the war drew on the experiences and the goals that they had set in the period mentioned above, hence, he is named the "Desert Fox" as a legacy.

Rommel came to final the domination exerted by his huge contributions as a "Ghost Soldier" during the French campaign. It was the "Ghost Division" success which was the first example of his expertise in the new style and played off the setting for further future success. Perfect teamwork was the ace with which he played the French campaign besides which he not only did show his strategic mind and the quality of his operation skills but also the ability to act innovatively facing a lot of stress besides. The features, formed at the time of his leadership in the "Ghost Division", would indeed make up the pillar of his military career and his legend as one of the greatest as well as the most esteemed military captains throughout the 20th century.

Rommel marketing the 7th Panzer Division was more than just a show of tactical ingenuity; it was an endorsement of his inspiring and effective as well as a good leader. His generalship during the French campaign was proof of his strategic acumen, operational proficiency, and, the ability to innovate under heavy pressure. These quality properties, developed during the periods of the control of the "Ghost Division," would always be the main definition of Rommel's military career and the basis of his legacy as one of the most reputable and influential military leaders of the 20th century.

Chapter 5

The Desert Fox

Rommel's Call to North Africa: The Birth of the Desert Fox

Time and again, Erwin Rommel was faced with the possibility of coming to grief, but listing among his tomb obliterations was not to be. The reason being that in early 1941 General Erwin Rommel was chosen to perform the duty that would remarkably raise his reputation in the military and even more importantly, thrust him into the category of great military leaders of all times. He was given the command of the Afrika Korps, a large body that had been just created, and later, he was ordered to shift his completely in a different direction to the African tropical region. His appointment to this special task, the "Desert Fox," was a direct consequence of his exceptional performance in France and his growing reputation for being the most innovative and interesting military leader in Europe. Time spent in North Africa was to be quite exceptional, different from his previous work in France. It required strategic acumen and adaptability beyond Rommel's exceptional batskills, which was what made it a true challenge.

The major strategic objective of Rommel was to support Mussolini's anti-British campaign in the region. It was so, especially when the Italian army was fighting a losing battle against British forces. The Italian armies that had quick breakthroughs at the beginning all the same were crushed again and again that the status became that of a backward situation in them. The British forces, having taken the opportunity of the Italian's vulnerable position, had already to a great extent made their way into the hostile territory. The situation of the Axis Powers in North Africa could not be more insecure; it was even arguable that they needed to have a commander who would come and unite them to become one. Rommel's victory in this new war zone was expected to make things better so that everybody else would also benefit from being associated with them.

When North Africa realized Rommel's arrival, he set his initial goal to bring the British offensive to a halt and to repose in the damaged Axis front line of defense. Rommel, whose leadership became very necessary, was appointed at a time when Italian forces had low morale and it was not clear if they could stand by for a long time. Rommel's leadership was expected to refresh the idea of the Axis by developing a successful campaign and therefore he had to bring a fresh mindset to the Anglo-Italian front.

The conditions in North Africa were completely unlike those that Rommel had ever dealt with in Europe. The vast, dry desert terrain was to bear unique logistical challenges including extreme temperatures, scarce water supplies, and difficult terrain for mechanized units. These environments, therefore, forced the Germans to come up with new methods of carrying out and supplying their war efforts. Rommel's resourcefulness and effective management of his resources were the deciding factors in his success in the desert.

The coming of Rommel to North Africa was characterized by his speed and the fact that he was very assertive and clear in his actions. He made a quick assessment of the situation, and his first move was implementation of his strategic plan. He made the first move in Operation Sonnenblume (Operation Sunflower) in February 1941. This operation focused on shoring up the Italian positions and creating a strong Axis presence in the area. The British were taken by surprise as a result of Rommel's aggressive maneuvers and his great skills at supplying and deploying his forces quickly which in turn forced their troops to stagnate.

Operation Sonnenblume was the appearance of a new era in mobile warfare with Rommel's innovative style. Using scouting and armored units, he was capable of carrying out rapid surprise attacks that destroyed British supply lines and communications. From Rommel's side, he remained fast and never rigid during the desert war, which caused him to see the British weak points, and he then took back some of the lost ground hence putting the British forces on the defensive.

Rommel did more with his upbeat and presence-in-the-moment approach to the conflict in the Desert. He was identified for his doer temperament, frequently walking on the front line and then making immediate decisions based on the immediate situation on the battlefield. The face-to-face interaction not only secured Rommel with an exact idea of the overall status but also motivated his troops. His frontline participation was a big shot in the arm for the men and, simultaneously, it gave them a sense of comradeship and loyalty leading to a strong unit.

Rommel's skilling of keeping the soldiers in good shape of conformity and unity was absolutely necessary in the heavy situation of North Africa. The kind of warfare carried out on the desert required the participation of forces to undergo great losses of the body and yet they had to remain highly motivated and focused. Rommel's charismatic leadership and his claim for the better life of his troops played a critical role in reaching these results.

His being posted to Africa also showed his tactical wisdom and his ability to practice the ideas of creativity. He saw that the movement and support are the main factors that feed the soldiering out at the desert (the movement and reserves of all the forces are main factors to nourish the soldiering at the desert). Thus, he concentrated on the control of strategic areas and supply lines, the ones which were cardinal in enhancing desert military operations. Rommel's focus on the instance of saving and the security of these assets guaranteed his soldiers' fight to be at that standard that pressed the British forces.

Apropos his duty as a commander in the North African battlefield was the capacity of Rommel to modify his strategies to meet the rapid and dynamic nature of desert warfare. Unlike on the western front in Europe, this kind of desert warfare quite a freight. The soldiers first make a rapid transition around the whole desert then they see each other. Rommel's knowledge of the matter and his ability to make quick and decisive moves ensured the spot of the enemy and thus maintained the initiative.

Rommel faced supply shortages, logistical difficulties, and the constant threat of British counterattacks, but his resolution and strategic foresight gave him the ability to overcome these challenges and his victory was significant. The command of Rommel in North Africa demonstrated his mastery of mobile warfare and establishment of an innovative military strategy.

Rommel's campaign in the first phase of North Africa built solid ground for his future achievements and he was established as a formidable force that the Allies could face. His capability to modify his approach to the unique problems of desert warfare together with his aggressive and flexible tactics soon led the tide of the war. Rommel's leadership during this time was characterized by his consistent pursuit of strategic objectives and his capacity to inspire and motivate his troops even under the harshest of conditions.

Rommel's appointment as the leader of the German Afrika Korps was a significant moment of his military career, which initiated his ascent to legendary status as the "Desert Fox." His distinctive way of adopting warfare, his dynamic leader type, and his skill to adapt to the harsh Norh African desert were the reasons for his success. Rommel's command not only saved the Axis position in North Africa but also it showed the world his exceptional skills in the war, which was very much necessary for the preparation of his achievements in the future. He is considered one of the greatest military leaders and the list of his legacies in military history is long.

Early Successes in the Western Desert

Blitz in the Desert: Operation Sonnenblume

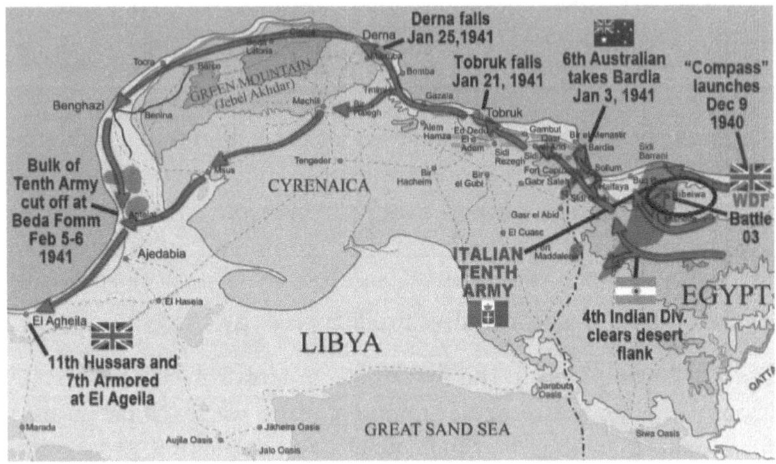

General Erwin Rommel turned things around in North African desert, establishing his Operation Sonnenblume (Operation Sunflower), a campaign that supported the fallen Italian forces and invaded Axis dominance into the region in May 1941. This operation was the advent of Rommel's formidable reputation as the "Desert Fox" because of his aggressive military skills, strategic wisdom, as well as his timely adaptation to the harsh desert conditions he encountered.

The Italian forces had gone through a bunch of disastrous failures at the hands of the British people, who had made significant advancements that made them capable of destroying the Axis powers from North Africa completely. The main target was to stop the British advance, strike back the enemy, and thus, Roman's personal mission was to re-strengthen the Axis forces aiming also to seal the axis front lines. The general's quick gaze at the battlefield, he quickly ordered the troopers to get going; his plan was already in motion to launch a counteroffensive that would surprise the British.

Rommel implemented the primary principles of a blitzkrieg campaign; quick response, and a resolute decision. He was able to grasp that surprise and speed were the only ways to outsmart the British, who with the absence of preparation could not face a breaking block. Rommel's iron-fist strategy was surprising not only to the British through the first series of guerilla warfare and at length owing to the offensive tactic was transformed into a defensive one.

Rommel's success in Operation Sonnenblume was partly due to the well-planned tactics of reconnaissance and armored units. Rommel was clever of the facts that doctrine showed the data allowing the appropriate command decisions whereas the intelligence paradise of the distance and sandy desert land over there required the highest of intelligence units of its kind. He released the expeditionary units to monitor the real-time data and the enemy's weaknesses in North Africa. To keep aware and unexpected, Rommel's decision was precisely to apply the information available in the attack. In prior attacks, they would hit from the places the bastion would be less likely to expect.

Rommel revolutionized the use of armour units in the same way. He took full advantage of the mobility and firepower of his tanks in order to carry out rapid and devastating attacks. This master strategist accomplished the feat of turning his reconnaissance data into useful information which was used for the purpose of countering the British forces by going around their lines and discovering the weaknesses in their defenses. Use of the armored car at such a speed and in such effectiveness was key to the return of the squad that had been escaping previously as well as to make the opponent played on the back foot.

The starting part of operation the Sonnenblume was characterized by a certain activity of the Rommel's forces in the desert. They were able to recapture some cherish positions and block the British supply lines. The fact that Rommel could keep the fast-moving units in close formation was a key factor that deterred the British army from regrouping and launching a counteroffensive. Through his relentless drive and tactical acumen, Rommel ensured that the Axis forces were the ones who dictated the engagement conditions and forced the British to react to his moves.

The leadership style of Rommel was of utmost importance for the successful operation of Sonnenblume. It was noted that he, many times himself leading the troops on the front line, we all equipped to make the appropriate choices at the right time so that the on-site war dynamics can be taken into account. Not only did his direct involvement in the case make it sure that General Rommel enjoyed an adequate comprehension of the realities but it also flattened an enthusiasm among the troops. The fact of having their commander with them on the frontline forced the soldiers to work as a team and at the same time, it was an element of motivation.

The large-scale event took place in the Libyan theater of war that made Rommel in the first place a master of the rapid and open conflict gauge. His mastery of the use of the agile attack with the clever use of surprise, speed as well as the reinforcement of the tactical fluidity of desert warfare became the typical standard of his command system. The insistence of Rommel on the maintaining of the offensive and the utilization of the chances that are given to him displayed his strategic talents and adaptability according to the nature of the fluid series of events, which desert fights may offer.

The example of Operation Sonnenblume also saw Rommel's creativity and risk-taking abilities. The wasteland created unique problems for the soldiers. His showing of means in the current was a mark to his genius as a warrior. His victory against the English forces in the face of these difficult was not only a sign of his capability as a military strategist but also his involvement in other events as his strategy was incredible.

But the development of Operation Sonnenblume went beyond the local-decisive triumphs. Rommel's success in the campaign had far-reaching strategic implications for the North African theater of operations. With the British stopped and recapture of lost territory, Rommel succeeded in creating a stable front for the axis and, thus, boosting morale for the Italian forces. The other side of the coin is that his triumphs symbolized the existing of the Axis power in North Africa, and hence were responsible to send a strong positive message to the British and Allied forces as well.

Rommel's command with his strong execution of Operation Sonnenblume was the prelude of his other campaigns in the Western Desert. The disaster was mainly due to British troops behavioral patterns that were too predictable. In this way, Rommel could outmaneuver the British and gain great success even in the midst of a serious shortage of tanks. Furthermore, the mission made Rommel have a tough fight as an enemy, and it was because of this that he is still one of the stalwarts and the best researcher of the general staffs in World War II.

The brilliant advancement of Operation Sonnenblume was the very first reason for Rommel's excellent military acumen. It was through various fashions like his aggressive behavior, the unique style of reconnaissance and armor, and his direct involvement that the vicissitudes came about. His main strength is being adaptive to almost an impassable place of the desert and then quickly managing to act fast. His work strategy was great and that is why he is often called the Desert Fox. This act not only defined the Axis but was also the building stone for Rommel's successful Western Desert years that made him famous as a modern war captain.

Encircling Tobruk: Rommel's Prolonged Siege

Tobruk had great strategic importance; it was not only located to the supply lines but also had a powerful defense. The fort and port were not only crucial strategic points for the British Victor Army that had proved to be very beneficial in terms of supplies and reinforcements. People were convinced that all was hopeless when Tobruk fell. Yet, the Tobruk siege did not last for long, it ended only when the British Empire was given the aid of complete confidence.

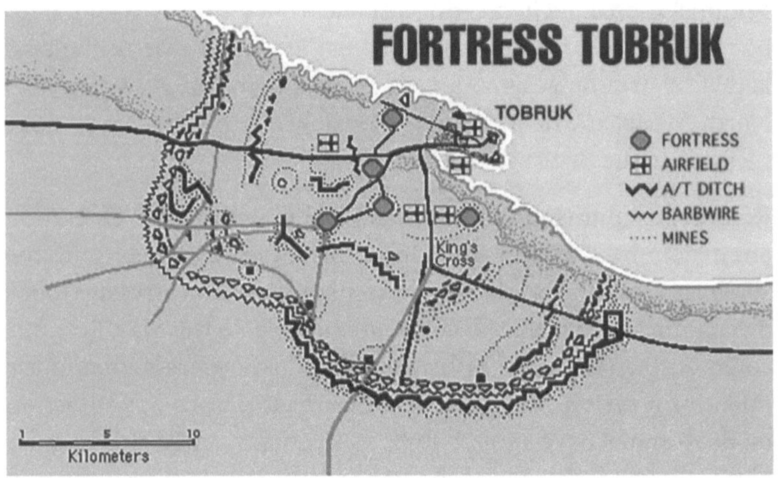

In this secluded area of security, Tobruk relied on two of the most important factors: the support of the Eighth British Army and the security of the fortress. However, the British troops managed to defend Tobruk against a siege, having been already prepared by reinforcing the positions and stocking up the needed supplies in order to confront a long-term war. Rommel's forces would face not only the detriment to British logistics, but also the moral weakness of the Axis force. "

For his part, Erwin Rommel started the bracketing of Tobruk impressively by perfect performance. So, his tanks, infantry and artillery, led to the isolation of the town, thus the enemy had no crossing. The town had been tethered by this surrounding action in order to crush the British defenders and compel them to escape to a less favorable position gradually. However, the British at Tobruk succeeded in getting a long-resistance due to a strong and prebuilt army reaction, notwithstanding the initial surround Tobruk was a remarkable point in the history.

The soldiers of the Allied forces in Torbruk, under the command of the Australian General Leslie Morshead, were very determined to keep the dock safe. They had underground forts and the harsh landscape of the desert as their allies, which made the Axis fail in their many attempts to take over the fort. The British troops and Tobruk allies from the Commonwealth showed great courage, as they came up with defensive techniques and just offensive moves that disturbed the result of Axis attempts of attacks.

Tobruk was the scene of a long-standing blockade that lasted for several months. This battle, which lasted for a long time, let us see the perseverance and strength of the soldiers of both, the besieged British garrison and Rommel's troops. Rommel's ability to hold on to Tobruk while dealing with other fronts clearly showed his strategic agility and determination. Although the situation was a deadlock, Rommel remained in his quest for strategy by devising and putting new tactics into action.

One of the main dilemmas that Rommel encountered in the desert during the siege was to allocate his resources and concentrate his guard on the various parts of the front. In addition to the constant siege of Tobruk, Rommel had to deal with the British who were trying to release the garrison and disrupt the supply lines of the Axis. The fact that Rommel had to be forever attentive to the sudden change and his gift of coming to grips instantly with the new conditions were the elements of his brilliant strategy. His adaptability was second to none.

Rommel's approach through the siege using his so-called 'combined arms' strategy aroused special interest in the experts. He combined the use of artillery with infantry assaults and tank infiltrations on the one side, targeting to destroy the resistance and create chances for breakthroughs. Nevertheless, the speciously strong and unusually spirited forces of Tobruk, who were always in trenches, did not allow these efforts to come to any success. The siege was a stalemate, both sides losing a great number of men and materials.

Albeit there were numerous difficulties, Rommel's guiding of the Tobruk siege was defined by his unshakeable resolve and his power to lift the spirit of his soldiers. His being in the front line and his tactics also cunning made the military stronger both physically and morally. The capacity of Rommel to hold out his troops at the ready, even under such harsh living conditions in the North African desert, was a proof of his outstanding leadership talents.

Actually, the extended siege brought about more opportunities for Rommel's troops to get the required supplies. The desert's logistics of a long-term siege involved a continuing influx of supplies, including food, water, ammunition, and fuel. Rommel's skill to handle these logistics even after the Allies had tried to attack his supply lines demonstrated his strategic planning and ingenuity in using resources. The ordinance he was using to stay in the battles fighter the tanks was the one that had the highest mobility and required the least amount of resources.

Although Tobruk was not taken immediately, the siege served as a case study for Rommel's siege warfare talent and showed the world his commitment to strategic goals despite the many blocks on the way. The long-standing fighting put both the besiegers and defense lines to the test, thus, it was clear that war in the desert was actually complicated. Rommel's ability to come up with new tactics and his insistence on Tobruk was praised and he was recognized as a master tactician and a strong-willed leader even after the failers tried to bring him low.

Tobruk's siege was not just a matter of the situation there but it also had a far-reaching effect on the war in North Africa. It took away the requisite amount of manpower and materials from both Axis and Allied forces, and thereby affected the military operation dynamics across the region. The release of Tobruk by British troops in December 1941 was the beginning of the road that led to victory, and though in its own right, it was a remarkable event that exposed Rommel's foresight and his strong survival skills in tough conditions.

"During the battle of Tobruk, his ethics were looked upon as his fightmanship nature, which was brave, smart, and never refused to stop." His skill that allowed him to deal with disadvantageous conditions in a well-organized way, keep the enemy forces enclosed at a high level and motivate his forces to fight against severe conditions, caused him to stick out and be remembered as the best military leader not only of the Second World War but in the entire history. The Tobruk siege, even though it ended in favor of the Allies, was clear evidence of Rommel's strategic wisdom and the unwavering commitment to the objectives he had set for himself that led to his being called the legendary "Desert Fox."

Key Battles and Campaigns

Battle of Gazala – The Left Hook Strategy

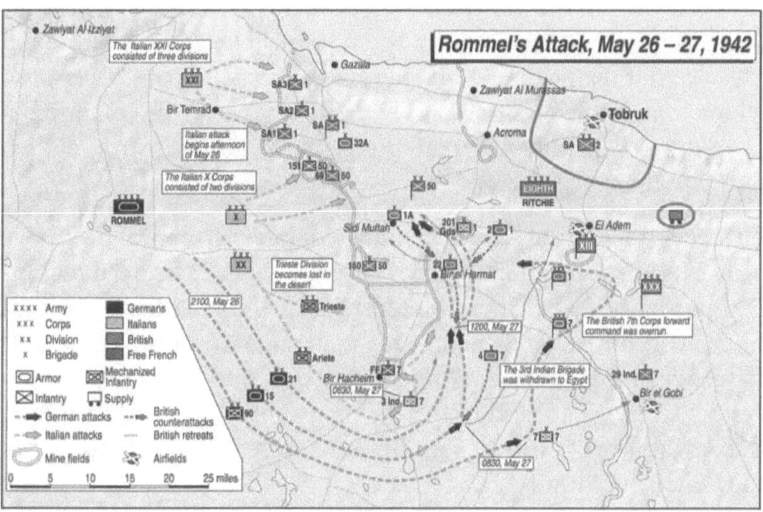

During the month of May and June 1942, the Battle of Gazala, the nickname which will last for centuries in history, was one of Erwin Rommel's North African campaign, the most brilliant and successful one. This fight was actually a sequence of clashes with maneuvers and countermaneuvers almost always taking the course of Rommel's outflanking and encircling of the British forces. Rommel's "left hook" method, which is a deep flanking movement that goes southwards, was the one that the British did not expect at all and the one that eventually disrupted their defensive plans. This situation created one of the decisive victories of the North African campaign of this genius field commander.

Rommel's strategic conception of the Battle of Gazala was basically held back by his vast knowledge of war strategies in the desert as well as by his inspiration to use the natural environment to his own advantage. The British Eighth Army, with General Neil Ritchie as the main commander, has created defensive positions along the Gazala Line, which runs from the Mediterranean southwards to the desert. Two defensive lines were positioned in these areas, equipped with many soldiers, so they did not let the other army pass. Nazis and the Italian divisions were the ones, which did not obey any order of the British and ran by them playing tricks. The British army put the mines all over, even on the flanks of the lighter lines. According to the remarks by Rommel, the above-mentioned idea was not really imaginative, and it was an anticipated operation which was unlikely to succeed. Subsequently, he planned a procedure to invade the rear positions of the British and then outflank them.

The very "left hook" strategy turned into an extremely brave move. Rommel decided to pilot the troops to the southern regions without crashing the main defenses of Britons and then to beat them to death in their area. This campaign is a thing that calls for exact timing, coordination, and also a good knowledge of the system to move around in the desert. Rommel's forces, including the Afrika Korps, and Italian divisions were in the vanguard and they finally did it safely and smartly.

While moving down the Britany coast Rommel's divisions experienced no resistance on the part of the British who failed to predict such an extensive manoeuvre by the enemy. The Afrika Korps speeded up moving to a great distance in a short time. The maneuver led to the destruction and disarray of the British units, which in their turn failed to face the danger, which was literally dropped on them. A thumb-up to victory in Libyan desert warfare and a thorough knowledge of speed and the element of surprise, as the basics were the capability of the military commander. These were the necessary qualities of the commander, and they were the very aspects of the battle he mastered.

One of the best periods of the battle was when Rommel's units attacked deep into the British territory. They were overrunning major positions and stumbling the supply lines. The Brits, who were suddenly confronted with the enemy's rear Axis forces, were totally amazed. He took advantage of their disorientation to the degree of keeping his ascendancy and then going on. His consistent application of such a combination of attacks, that included tanks, infantry, and artillery, allowed him to keep the enemy troops under pressure and kept them from retreating.

One of the most notable battles of the Battle of Gazala was inferring the battle for the stronghold referred to as the "Cauldron." Rommel's troops could siege a huge part of the British Eighth Army and lock them in an ischemic pocket that subjected them to the assaults without cessation. The British, however fervently they fought to escape out of the encircling, relented in their efforts in the fact of the exhaustive attack by the loots of Rommel. The Axis soldiery, in their brave fighting and undeterred determination, did their enemies in the eyes with the gradual developments that led to the closing of the spaces which the trapped British army occupied.

In the Battle of Gazala, Rommel's showing off of his brilliant strategy, rapid and undoubted achievements were seen. The British were caught off balance as his troops deliberately moved deep into the enemy's lines, provoking chaos and panic. The high speed and the volume of Axis attacks were so great that the British defense lines fell before they noticed, and essentially all British troops and equipment were further captured, bringing the battle to a victorious conclusion. The Eight Army heavily disarmed with the loss of these resources had to obey in the urge to step back first and then gather the forces.

The Gazala triumph was not only a demonstrated strategic victory in war but also a part of strategic triumph. It showed that Rommel was a visionary who skillfully adjusted every maneuver on the field to suit the particular circumstances and the opposing army. The "left hook" maneuver, Rommel's new defensive approach, detracted the British who had to emphasize that offensive strategy over the defensive one, and it also unveiled his strategic capabilities of being deceitful and surprising his opponents. Rocmell's success at the place solely proved his mind-blowing tactician skills and which won the hearts or even admiration of both allies and opponents alike.

After Gazala, the situation of North African campaign was very different and long-lasting. That defeat made the British to pull back into the lines of defense around El Alamein, which was the scenario for the next battles to come in the region. Rommel's triumph at Gazala energized the Axis armies, and it gave them a sense that Rommel was the best general they ever had. This battle also illustrated the ideal performance of blitzkrieg operations in the may area where the desert environment is such that the effectiveness of these tactics was based on mobility and rapidity.

The more retreat became known as the Battle of Gazala showed Rommel's deep and clear understanding of the warfare's principles that he could masterfully adapt to the challenges of the North African theater. By being always near, instead of just sending instructions, he showed his form of leadership, which in turn prompted the people as well as the completion of the vision he had outlined. The battle demonstrated that Rommel could read the big picture clearly and then implement tactics accurately, a feature of his military genius.

Gazala Battle is still the proof of Rommel's great powers as a military commander. His desire to blow it out, as well as his use of nuance and deception and his relentless aim for victory even in the provocatively challenging conditions, made him one of World War II's greatest tacticians. "The left hook" is one of the strategies that stand out a lot for being a great example of military strategy that the homeland and the other countries went through to together in fixing it through the war.

Rommel's victory in Gazala in the Nazi campaign of Africa sparked off a turning point in the nature of the campaign making it a more mobile campaign from then on, and setting the stage for the future engagements. The experiences gained from this fight are even now researched and appreciated by military history and strategy writers, however, the lasting importance of Rommel's achievements in the Westen Desert is indicative of them demonstrating that.

Turning the Tide: The First Battle of El Alamein

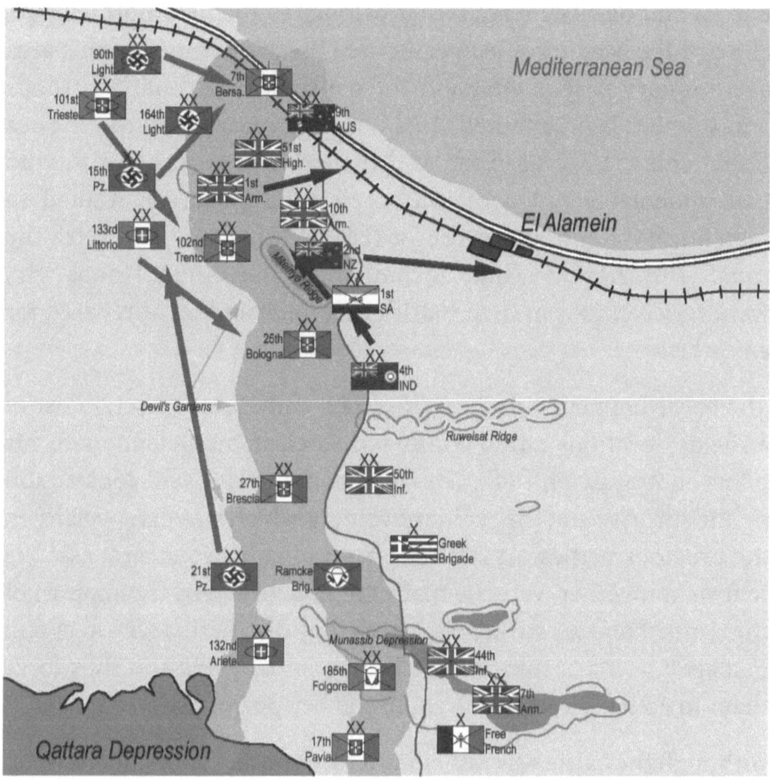

Erwin Rommel, following his most spectacular triumph, that is, the Battle of Gazala, he pushed and passed Egypt on his way to the Suez Canal to have the control of it, and so the Axis forces could have a strategic advantage. The Suez Canal is the strategic part of communication between the Allies that, if they occupy it means that they cut the connections between other countries of the Allies and get new weapons of war for themselves. All the same, the British managed to stop Rommel's first attempt to take over the Suez Canal in July 1942. This struggle of power has been proved as a pivotal event in the conflict of Northern Africa, when the British forces, under the guidance of General Claude Auchinleck, stopped Rommel's invasion in the end of all despite the heavy losses of men.

As we have known, the First Battle of El Alamein played out on the barren and desolate terrain that belongs to the near north Egypt, close to the Mediterranean seashore. The significance of this area as a military base is vital and the constant flow route for troops and supplies is maintained. This hot spot was a portal to the Suez Canal and the Middle East, and the German Africa Corps, who had undeniably just achieved a resounding success, wanted to march ashore and attack the British Eighth Army and seize the canal. This, however, had no impact on the British troops who were very cautious in their battle equipment and well prepared for any attack.

The battle happened on June 30, 1942, and Himmler sent a list of airfields' locations and a command to clear the defenders to his pilots on August 14, 1942. The strategy of the Luftwaffe took action on the surprise and the rapid movement which was his specialty in the previous battles. At the very beginning, various tank assaults that went together were the main thing, followed by the support of the ((mm)) and air strikes. Heavy as they did, Rommel's forces still managed to make some of the British initial gains and thus force them to go back and even to grab the key positions.

Although the battle was rather hard for Rommel to further develop his offensive and the logistical difficulties that are faced when carrying out a campaign in the desert, yet the battle demonstrated Rommel's shortcomings. The first sign of weakness was that the supply shortages started to take a toll on the Axis forces. Their supply routes in sympathy with their bases located in Libya led to the increased losses in fuel, bullets, and other essentials. The troops of Rommel's who had been worn out by the immediate and continuous conflicts, additionally, they were also showing signs of fatigue and logistic strains.

The resolute fierceness of the British Eighth Army became one more adversity for Rommel. Despite being strained and worn out the soldiers kept their stand. The British artillery was the most effective in this occasion and managed to discourage Rommel a lot, and that caused many deaths with the passing of the Axis troops. The well-placed mines with the fortified positions were stopping Rommel's advancement and so, they caused him a considerable amount of trouble.

The Rommel's inability to breakthrough the British strongpoint became clear. The Axis soldiers had to take a step back and change their composure because they were stimulated by the supply deficits. The Englishmen, becoming aware of the diminished rebel's blocking ability, did an about-face they counterattacked to recover the lost ground and strengthen their positions. While they had significant casualties, those counterattacks nonetheless toppled more of Rommel's defences and kept him from pulling off any full-blown Axis assaults.

In the initial battle, the strategic problems of Rommel being able to ensure the logistics needed for the move over long supply lines showed up by the First Battle of El Alamein. Harsh desert environment strikingly intensified logistical difficulties, therefore, the shortening of offensives became virtually impossible. The battle showed the necessity of limp free supply paths and if they are not taken then it resulted in the impact of the logistics that led to the military operation failure. The military disciplines of the two enemies were not enough for the Germans to compensate for their flaws very enough which led to the failure of the first attack.

The British Eighth Army's resolve and will to fight back was the main reason the Germans failed to advance. Auchinleck's dynamic leadership, which was shown his ability to learn and adjust to the dynamic battlefield surroundings, was very influential in British defense. The British military's turn-the-other-cheek approach and quick responses enabled the troops to get out of sticky situations and make the right moves.

The upshot of the battle was that the North African campaign was greatly affected. The stymying of Rommel's advance at El Alamein signified the conclusion of the Axis forces' dominant sway in this region of the conflict. It gave the Allies a much-needed boost in their spirits and an opportunity to come together and consolidate their positions. The First Battle of El Alamein was the decisive battle for the coming battles, such as the Second Battle of El Alamein, where the Allies would firmly triumph and thus initiate to change the course of the North African campaign.

Rommel's first experience at the First Battle of El Alamein showed that his method had a limit and that logistics and supply played a crucial part in war. The fight displayed that the most brilliant plans and the most tenacious leading could be destroyed by logistical constraints and enemy resistance that exists already. Rommel's capacity to adjust to these challenges and get knowledge from this event would impact his strategies and decisions in the future.

The First Battle of El Alamein stands as a significant chapter in the history of World War II, it shows the relationship of strategy, logistics, and leadership in deciding the outcomes of military engagements. Rommel's offensive was not only stopped by tactical flaws; rather, it was a combination of operational problems, and the British forces' fortitude. It still stands as proof of the complexity of combat and the numerous aspects that operate on its course.

The Turning Point: The Second Battle of El Alamein

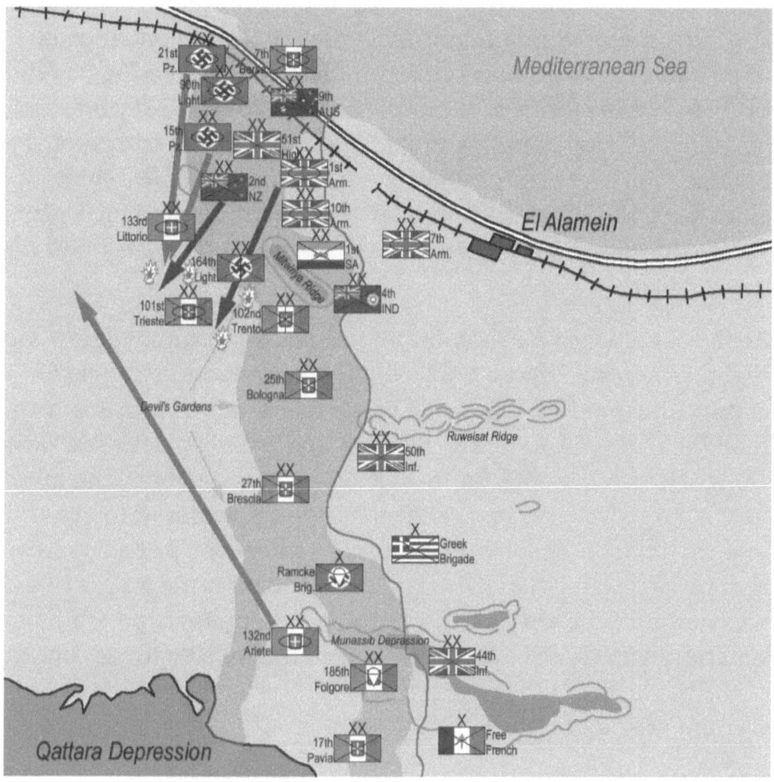

The Second Battle of El Alamein lasted from October 23 to
November 11, 1942, and was a decisive fight that signified
Rommel's defeat in the North African arena. General Bernard
Montgomery who replaced the former commander, was the one
who organized this fight, his plan was to use all his resources and
another reinforcement to attack the opponents and force them to
give up their positions, Then the British troops who were in great
danger began to take the leading positions and destroy the goals
of the enemy in turn, The outcome of this battle was a pass of time
that the North African zone where Axis power was at its peak and
the successful retreat of Rommel's forces.

After the loss of Tobruk, Erwin Rommel's own troops knew that the good tie between Rommel and his forces was broken. This new attention implied more air and sea attacks on their supply lines and thus the continuation of their fuel, ammunition, and other important material imports was progressively decreasing. He did his best, but his forces were not sufficient to the task of protecting his rear and supplying his units. Even though the troops of the opponent answer were making sure the supplies came to him, the allies with their superior numbers and carefully designed plans and a continuous supply of reasures were ready to punish him for that mistake.

At the time, when he took on the role of the commander of the Eighth Army in August 1942, Montgomery had to struggle for a couple of months to prepare for the operation. He, in his turn, thought that way to break through the enemy's defenses were along the lines, would be to use heavy weapons but remember not to forget to use the breach followed by armored forces and infantry attacks. There is a critical case where the British strategy is more successful than the German one, namely the weight of the numbers and the amount of planning and organization are more superior in the British troops. This, of course, related to the context of the battle and is the reason the maneuvering from the German account was not as successful.

The battle got rolling on October 23, 1942. The soldiers started the fight with the artillery bombardment on-axis defense positions at night. The operation aimed to remove all the minefields that the Germans were protecting with and make paths for the British soldiers to get to the Germans. There was the first infantry charge next, when the British forces who kept moving under the favour of dark to the Axis soldiers in camp to which they would be in disbelieve. Though avidly resisted, the British managed to take over a couple of main positions and establish themselves in the Axis fortresses.

Rommel who had been out of the field for some time because he was weak due to illness returned rapidly and took over the command. His troops after the defeat assembled a series of counter-attacks in hopes to secure the British assault and restore the fortification of their defense lines. The war turned into a savage bloodshed of attrition, with both sides having a lot of losses. The fighting provoked not only the death of many soldiers but also trained the strength and resolution of both armies in the rough desert conditions.

The Britains kept applying fighting pressure on the Axis positions as time went on. Montgomery, who brought a process of cleaning off all the minefields with infantry, resulting in large numbers of tanks being blown away in his wake, discovered that his strategy was working effectively. The Axis forces, even with their strong resistance, were gradually kicked out. The Brits, thanks to their more and strength in supplements, as well as a smart act of the unit, can be remembered; they left Rommel's men a little the worse for wear by these well-executed maneuvers.

One of the key moments, the day when Operation Supercharge was launched, was on November 2, 1942. The phase of the offensive was to strike at the Axis in a way so much concentrated with tanks and infantry that in no time by this axe, the Germans would be striving to escape it in that direction, they had barely any resistance. The strong offensive romped the front line of the Axis leading them to have big losses and the missing of the lines making it harder for them to hold a coherent line of defense.

Rommel, to acknowledge the urgently desperate, made an attempt to set rules for leading a retreat so he could pull as many of his soldiers as possible out of the danger. Nevertheless, the continuous threat from the British and the constant endurance of Montgomery's forces made the situation harder and harder for their men. The Axis soldiers, because of the lack of fuel and ammunition, were disadvantaged in coordinating the withdrawal and faced challenges to do it. The destruction of many military units meant that they left behind an assortment of weapons and this brought more disharmony and confusion.

Rommel's flight after the ever so ignominious defeat of the Axis in the Battle of El Alamein signified the initiation of the Axis withdrawal from the North African area. The confrontation substantially altered the strategic dynamics of the region. It was this confrontation that shattered the belief that the desert wastelands protected the Axis and only the Allies could be expected to rise to their full potential. The collapse of Rommel's resistance to El Alamein, as well as the Allied invasion of North Africa under Operation Torch in November 1942, indicated a turning point in the area's power balance.

Even though Rommel was a genius strategist and a man of influence over his followers too, he could not balance the qualitative and quantitative superiority of the Allies. El Alamein II clearly illustrated how critical logistics and supply were in modern war. Because the Axis were not able to sustain their supply lines and provide their positions with enough reinforcements, they lost in North Africa.

Additionally, the battle was a show to remind the people of the world that the highly planned and orderly approach of Monty to fighting was absolutely correct The policy of preparation, coordination and building a lot of force, was provided as the main factors that resulted in Monty's penetration of the Axis' stronghold. His guidance throughout the battle was brought out of his capability to stay his mind and hold a tough regime over the soldiers that might stop them from following the plan with enough exactness.

The Second Battle of El Alamein was a major victory in the North African war that showed a turning point in history. It was the first time Rommel could not achieve his offensive goals in the region, and it signalled the beginning of the decline of the Axis in North Africa. The fight proved that the key to military success is logistics, planning, and coordination. It also brought out the strong defenses of the British Eighth Army under Montgomery's leadership.

The Axis forces were in full retreat in the wake of the battle, with the Allies chasing them toward Libya and eventually Tunisia. The victory of El Alamein became their North African entrance, and further troop movements would make them win the desired expulsion of Axis forces from the continent. The battle is a monument to the strategic and operational skills of both Montgomery and Rommel, and it draws the attention to the complexities and difficulties of desert warfare.

The Second Battle of El Alamein, the ones that destroyed never to rise again, is the gravestone and the resurgence of the Axis who wanted to continue is a whole other issue. The defeat of Rommel's Afrika Korps showed the end of their efforts in North Africa, which set the platform for Allied victory in the Mediterranean theater. The teachings of this war no one can dispute are still the subject of the researchers of military history and strategy, implying its enduring place in the battle of military tales.

The Desert Fox: Rommel's Legacy in North Africa

On the other hand, Erwin Rommel went to North Africa and defeats the Western Desert and these were the key parts of his brilliant years in the army. This particular period, marked by mastermind plans and bold moves, led to his recognition as one of the best military leaders on the planet during the Second World War. Through his resourcefulness in dead, the barren desert was his playground, and he was able to perform literally a sprint for miles. His mobile warfare tactics and the way he handled desert conditions were some of the characteristics that marked him as the most extraordinary "Desert Fox."

The escapade of Rommel in North Africa started with the Sonnenblume Action that was carried out in February 1941. Rommel, having been charged with the duty of steadying the shaky Italian front and stopping the British' advance, displayed his mastery of battle tactics in no time. His fierce opposition counterattack, which took the British by storm, allowed them to reclaim the lost land and ensure a firm grip of the Axis in the region. This launching showed Rommel's capability to perform such rapid and decision operations, acting as a platform for his progressive achievements in the future.

One of Rommel's early major successes in the war was the Assult of Tobruk which began in April 1941. The town of Tobruk was a needfully supply port for the British and it was captured by the Germans for controlling supply lines in the region. Rommel's troops marched around the city, covering its defenders in a blanket of despair as no reinforcement or supplies were possible. Without his sector, Rommel's relentless assault proved his strategical skills. During the engaging period of the siege, which went on for a few months, was the opportunity for the Axis and British to know each other's ability to stand the difficulties, it was outstanding in the fortitude of Rommel's aspiration for the strategic objectives through the challenging obstacles.

Rommel was a genius at the Battle of Gazala, which was in May and June 1942. "Left hook" tactics were used by him in the desert sides by which Rommel cut off British soldiers from the reinforcement of their defences and thereof disrupted the British attack on his artillery. Rommel's knowledge to go deep behind the British lines caused much confusion and disorder and this led to the capture of a large number of British troops and equipment. This Battle proved to be Rommel's dominance of artillery tactics in the desert and his perfect mastery of executing complicated and risky operations in the waste heat across the Libyan territories.

On the other hand, the First Battle of Alamein was the turning point in the campaign in North Africa in July 1942. Amongst his past victories, Rommel's power was too weak, and his warriors, who were also faced with serious%logistical problems, had been seriously overexerted, the British were under General Claude Allowance and they had been able to stop Rommel's rescue. In other words, a lost battle showed that things were not same for him in the offensive and he was experiencing strategic challenges mainly because of having the campaign sustained in such rough desert conditions. The Eighth Army of the English and the fused strong defensive shafts they were able to put on bakzard to Rommel, turned out to be one of the major reasons for the failure of Rommel's advancement.

The concluding part of Rommel's African campaign was the Second Battle of El Alamein, together with both its periods in October and November 1942. General Bernard Montgomery's British Eighth Army began a well-organized and well-armed attack on Rommel's crowded positions. His tactical sense along with devotion to his soldiers can't be denied but nevertheless, Rommel's soldiers, who became too weak due to missing material supply and tiredness could no longer hold off the strong material and the difference in logistics of the Allied Force. The fightings and movements in a definite stage of the battle finally led to a resounding victory of the Allies, as a result of the struggle Rommel was forced to move across the western direction and the countdown of the Axis leaving the North African terrain had started.

The impact of the battles that Rommel conducted in North Africa, even if they were not always successful, remained perpetual in the history of the military. His quick decision making and continuous pressure for objectives showed his hard work and the pursuit of victory. It is not enough to say that his tactical maneuvering skill was the best, he was also recognized as a solid warrior because of his warpath with the strategic objectives. Rommit's generalship style that is known by his experiential approach and his ability to motivate his soldiers to great extents, was tramonitor to success against the so often crushing of chances.

Rommel's North African military conquest legacy goes way beyond mere field triumphs. His employment of innovative combined arms tactics, infantry, armor, and air support being part of them, had an influence on modern military doctrines and the developing process of the swift mobile warfare strategies. Rommel's stress on fast takes and unexpectability of operations and the use of blitzkrieg methods in the desert air made it very clear that the flexibility of the military learning curve was nonnegotiable in the war time.

Rommel's exploits also highlighted logistics' role as a pivot factor in contemporary military operations. The problems he encountered while trying to keep his supply lines safe and ensure the flow of important resources were the main factors that determined the outcomes of battles. The problems of the desert wars of attrition showed the straitjacket of the idea fof having safe and speedy logistic routes that was a striking lesson of strategic executive and modern military planning that still holds today.

In North Africa, despite the fact that the Axis forces managed to defeat eventually, Rommel's decisive victories have influenced and earned him a place in the hall of fame of the best military strategists and tacticians. Rommel's agility in desert combat and his courageous and innovative style of warfare that made him stand out as one of the most influential military leaders in his era was there. The campaigns of Rommel in the Western Desert not only displayed his tactical genius but also evidenced his born strategic thinker and his clear grasp of the larger picture of military actions.

The Second Battle of El Alamein is the one that particularly becomes the proof of the decisive moments in World War II, and it symbolizes the downfall of Axis intentions in North Africa, leading to the victory of the Allies in the Mediterranean theater. Rommel's capability to gain knowledge from his trials and forces and to modify his mechanisms according to the variations of situations is an inalienable feature of his influence on military command and strategy.

When contemplating on Rommel's North African campaigns, it is obvious that his legacy in military history is long skate in the battles. His memory as the "Desert Fox" remains a positive force for soldiers and historians as it sheds light on the subtleties and difficulties of wars. Rommel's accomplishments in North Africa remain a symbol of great tactical and strategic skills, thus, the overall significance of his contribution to the art of war, therefore, is undeniable.

Chapter 6

Strategic Challenges and Administrative Acumen

Logistics of War: Rommel's Struggles in the Desert

None sounded more than the issues of logistics and supply that struck not a few campaigns of Erwin Rommel had to face in the North African desert. Thousands of hot and dry beautiful areas and unfriendly soil made the regular supply of stores such as gas, bullets, provisions, and water uphill. The German troops were exposed to enemy action quite literally, relying as they did on supply chains that extended along the coast of Mediterranean Libya. On the other hand, desert warfare infused the logistical problems faced by the German commander, Rommel, with a multinational aspect.

The logistics problems were additionally aggravated by the effects of the Allied forces who attacked Rommel's supply lines by air and sea quite often. These attacks left the supply routes in shambles, which caused the Afrika Korps to operate with reduced efficiency levels due to the lack of proper cargoes. The fierce determination of the Allied forces to block Rommel's supplies made the logistics an additional and relentless battleground, a war which was as important as the one fought during the actual combat encounters.

To help in the context, the lack of infrastructure in North Africa was a major deterrent to smooth logistics. The environment was even more of a drawback for efficient transportation. The shortage of good roads and railway lines meant that the transport of weapons had to be made across rough and often impassable paths. The use of truck lines to bring in materials across the vast terrain in the desert became more complicated and weaker. The convoys were bothersome, slow-moving, and were the prey of opposing planes. The continuous fear of airplanes coming and attacking became a reason why Rommel conceptualized original ways that could protect and sustain his supply lines.

Rommel's ability to face these logistics bottlenecks was one of the trademarks of his leadership. Rommel was very skillful in using Allied supplies to the utmost to assist his forces efficiently. This adaptability was critical in promoting the operational capability of the Afrika Korps despite the various logistic problems. Rommel's prowess in redirecting and deploying the captured equipment and resources to different objectives was his brilliant resourcefulness as well as strategic foresight.

The chief logistics concern that Rommel had to deal with was the transportation of fuel. In the desert, fuel was not only necessary for the movement of vehicles; it was the lifeblood of the whole operation. Tanks, trucks, and other armored vehicles would be stranded, making it impossible for the Afrika Korps to move without enough fuel. The long supply lines meant that fuel had to be transported over great distances, often through areas vulnerable to Allied interdiction. The insufficiency of fuel reserves often checked Rommel's actions, thus logistics appeared to be a decisive component of the strategic process.

The supply of ammunition was another significant problem. The requirement of constant supply of ammunition was that it should be supplied in great quantities and within the shortest time possible for the fighters to keep up the offensive. On the other hand, the preparation and storage of large quantities of ammunition were subject to the harsh desert environment and restricted fuel availability, thus leading to frequent ammo shortages. Rommel had to be very judicious in his use of ammunition, as he singled out the most critical things to his need and saved them wherever possible. This required highly precise planning and intimate knowledge of the tactical requirements of each battle.

The supply of food and water was an equal obstacle. The severe desert environment caused the water sources to be restricted and contaminated most of the time. A constant fight to get the required drinking water to the troops resulted in the health and morale of Rommel's troops being affected. Food deliveries also involved the transportation of products over a long distance, this being a constant issue of logistics for both their quality and quantity. The difficult environmental conditions made it hard for the men as well as the equipment, with the scorching heat and the sands affecting the efficiency of the equipment.

Rommel showed his insight in logistics also at the level of strategic planning of the most important innovation. Often, he was taken with the idea of seizing opposing depots and still taking advantage of their resources when they were his enemies. Via this method, not only did it relieve some of the logistic giants but also it cut off the enemy's supply lines. He was able to include these supplies that he got from his s out-size his reach into his supply chain and that was evidence of his logistics intelligence and military tactics as a commander in the army.

Nevertheless, this demonstration was unable to change the fact that of the service stress stayed as the mainstay throughout Rommel's activities in North Africa. Conditions such as lack of fuel, ammunition, food, and water deeply influenced his activities. The troubles related to supplies were not confined to the movement of goods, they were also related to the maintenance and operation of the forces in a state of readiness and effectiveness under the extreme conditions.

The interplay of logistics and tactics in Rommel's North African campaigns is an exemplary case of the vital role of the supply chain in modern warfare. It has been observed that the capacity of logistics to sustain efficiency is as significant as personal skills and tactics on the battlefield. Rommel's adventures in North Africa stress the intricacies and predatory nature of military logistics, where the possible success of the operation could depend on the ability to ensure a steady flow of necessary resources.

Rommel's logistic problems also prove the fact that the Axis powers in North Africa had to deal with the major tactical issues. The region's geographical and infrastructural constraints, along with the never-ending Allied impacts, developed an environment very hard for sustained military operations. The war of life and death to get and keep supply lines safe was a feature that created many other patterns and influenced the outcomes of the main battles of the North African campaign.

As a result of the logistics and supply problems Erwin Rommel suffered the worst period in his military career while operating in the North African desert. His personal ability to approach these restrictions and his smart utilization of the used captured Allied items indicated his resilience and strategic vision. Nevertheless, the always increasing logistic load only managed to underscore the weak points and the dangers of his strategy. Rommel's stories prove the dominance of logistics in battle and the long-term effect of supply chain management on military strategy and operation achievement.

Desert Warfare Redefined: Rommel's Tactical Innovations

Rommel's operations in Africa, exceptionally hard as the army's innovation was, stood out as if it had become a routine behavior of his due to his continual attempts to add new value to the war.

Rommel's desert campaigns (132- day Campaign) in North Africa, though extremely challenging as far as logistics were involved, were honored for his revolutionary ideas on desert warfare. His profound knowledge of desert fighting conditions, on the one hand, allowed him to create and apply tactics and strategies that excelled his side while taking advantage of the enemy's sides' weaknesses, on the other hand. These inimitable strategies were not only manifested in the mastering of technical questions as well as supported by the use of the state-of-the-art technology. One cannot but recognize the creative spirit of Field Marshal Rommel and his indomitable will which resulted in the creation of such tactics. His might was the real key of success during the battle of tremendous technological development and organized warfare. His achievements in mobile warfare, as well as other innovative tactics, indeed prove Rommel's extraordinary talents not only in conducting organized masses of armored units efficiently but also in his astonishing account of those plus many more during the harsh desert conditions.

Rommel was the first to adopt the innovative concept of mobile warfare, known also as blitzkrieg tactics, in the desert. The application of the blitzkrieg system, exemplified by the highest speed and the quickest changes of direction on the part of the attacking side in order to disturb the enemy through these tactics and the surprise element of it all, was just the right thing for the development of the North African regions. By driving the tanks at incredible speeds and by changing the direction of their movements, Rommel achieved the strategic advantage of outdoing the British initiated forces into the unconsciousness of the enemy. Working in this manner Rommel managed to outflank and encircle the hostile parties creating confusion and interrupting the plans of the defenders who failed to protect the positions of theirs.

Linking the main point of his message with the enemy's weakest spot, he took up a firmer position to be more specific, so Rommel's forces could have a more clear goal to strike off successfully. With the desert serving as a battalion only, and with such open and vast expanses of the terrain, it was almost impossible to find proper natural defensive positions. Rommel decided to take advantage of the desert's openness by keeping an operational tempo at its highest level, keeping his forces always moving, and never getting a time to set up a defensive line. Rommel's fast-driving movements around the desert were key to the efficient management of battle and establishing the norms of the engagements that were not known to the enemy. He was able to utilize his brilliance in the sudden initiative gained, catching the British forces, who were often dumbly protected.

Successfully launching surprise attacks in the desert required precise planning and coordination. Rommel's troops were experts at the execution of operations which were fast, flexible, and caught the enemy off guard. These operations frequently took place right into the enemy territory, which were executed through rapid seizing of the breaches of the defence lines. Rommel's ability to respond to the dynamics of desert warfare and his determined pursuit of the operation objectives were key to the successful manoeuvres.

Aside from Blitzkrieg, Rommel was the first who introduced combined arms tactics for the desert. He figured out that successful integration of various branches of military—infantry, tanks, artillery, and air support—was crucial to the winning of decisive battles. Rommel's method was based on bringing these different elements together, so that they could act together and shift the pressure from one front to another one frequently.

The integration of the infantry and armoured forces enabled Rommel to benefit from the strengths of both. When tanks broke through enemy lines, they were able to do it with speed and firepower; actually, the infantry followed the tanks immediately and blocked and held the obtained positions. This integrated military way led to Rommel's forces continuing their advancements and solidifying the gains. Artillery was the main weapon which was used for shelling enemies and attacking no matter if they were moving or not, while air support provided additional fire power and also carried out reconnaissance tasks.

Rommel's ability to coordinate these different elements and execute complex operations showed his tactical adoration and adaptability. The flexibility of the movie, "flexibility is not included," was like this, and the United States only being hit confirmed the promise to place the ship in different countries, but the other cars are shipped in Vietnam due to its out of stock situation. The possibility of executing such an operation was vital when it came to the desert, a place where the front lines are in an abstract condition and the roads are so far that there can be no definite plan but on the contrary a lot of constant swerving and improvisation.

Rome was able to find his creative way to bring new things into Africa by sending his reconnaissance and intelligence services. Exhibiting an impressive military tactic, Rommel used reconnaissance and gained the most accurate and fastest information possible. He deployed the specially trained IDF soldiers to inspect and carry information about the positions, movements, and capabilities of the enemy. Mostly, the information was used for planning and executing his operations wherein the German General detected an enemy's weakness in defence and took the chance to strike.

Rommel being different in his logistic methods in the North African campaign was also a factor. Despite having the usual problems related to logistics, he was again clever not only so that his forces would be still operational but the last supply points would be hit to good effect. In this specific one, the main means he used to obtain almost the same operational capability despite restrictions of logistics was the production of the necessary soldiers.

It was the effectiveness of the new ideas of Rommel on desert warfare that directed the North Africa campaign. His ability to maneuver at tremendous speed and his careful application of the combined-arm tactics in addition to the British forces were the main factors contributing to the significant successes he scored in these battles. Succeeding these ploys became not only a morale boost for Axis soldiers, but it also indicated the potentiality of modern, quick-action warfare in such a region.

Nevertheless, His innovations in the army also exposed (pointed out) the limitations and weaknesses of his methods. The high operational pace and the primary reliance on mobility imposed heavy pressures on the commodity chains, causing the persistent logistical problems, which, in turn, became a serious barrier in efforts to hold assaults. The need for continuous movement and the tough desert climate damaged not only vehicles but also people, and when the eventual Allied attack was executed at El Alamein, security logistics and continued help were attributed with the victory.

Rommel was a genius in desert warfare as he came up with innovative ways of dealing with the situation. Through his exceptional skills and the introduction of modern tactics and methods of approach, Rommel carved a niche for himself as the most influential military commander of World War II in Africa. These principles may be observed in the present military practice and his role as a pioneer in the field is also evident as well.

Looking at Rommel's artefacts (innovations) in desert warfare, it comes out clear his contributions transcended the near area of the North African war. His adoption of blitzkreig warfighting concept, where he relied on rapid movements, surprise tactics, and adaptability, was the deciding factor in the modern-day military tactics. The aggressiveness and sheer modernity of his concept though a northeastern African campaign is a good example of careless thinking, and it being said that he missing the opportunity to seize and use the assets of then overfleet.

Coalition Command: Rommel's Relationship with Italian Allies

One of the most delicate and complicated problems Erwin Rommel had to solve in the North African battles was the relationship with his Italian allies. The Axis forces in the region were composed of German and Italian troops, and the cooperation between them was the key to the effective application of the strategy. Clearly, the exchange of plans within the Axis camp, mostly the issue between Rommel and the Italian commanders, was a thorny sign of the Axis campaign against the enemy.

The Italians who were the force to create the highest level of troop numbers yet they were in dip position in term of equipment and the training was the key difference from the Germans. In this context, Rommel was quite often annoyed with the slow and messy functioning of the Italian forces, which happened due to low performance and of a certain reliability in the Italian soldiers. Additionally, the Italian soldiers noted logistical and operational challenges, for instance, the cumbersome provision of arms and the insufficiency of necessities. The problems had to be dealt with; Rommel could not care whether the forces were not strong enough, he was concerned about the priority of displaying a united front. So, he century the revival collaboration with the Italians.

Rommel's diplomacy and his power to inspire soldiers' confidence and loyalty were also very much in control of these relationships. Demandingly, he used his dominant character and hands-on approach, and as a result, the Italian soldiers expressed their sympathy by liking his courageous act of being with them in the combat. His way of teaching soldiers by example was the most important move that a leader can show to his units. Sometimes, Rommel would bravely take such personal risks as he considered the Italians' backing crucial for the prosperity of his global strategic goals. The Italians, by having a better perception of themselves and having time to proactively engage with the enemy, were cornerstone rationally of their support to the Rommel's campaign.

One of the key challenges Rommel faced was the differing strategic priorities and operational approaches between the German and Italian leadership. The Italian commanders, who were working under the direction of their superiors in Rome, often had to pursue other priorities and were restrained by different directives from Rommel in Berlin. These differences occasionally resulted in disagreements and conflicts over the right way to go. The rebel Rommel's one-sided character alongside his practice of jumping to the side roads when necessary worsened the situation between the two factions.

Nevertheless, Rommel impressed his gift of negotiation when he settled the disputes with a wonderful demonstration of love. He proactively promoted The main idea was the joint efforts of the axis powers versus the Allied forces in the battle of the war. Rommel's strategies in the period were irredeemably tied with these positive developments. Rommel's initiatives of integrating the Italian troops into his modus operandi were the backbone of the Union and the overall cohesion in the Axis North African forces. He realized that he could win his campaign only when his troops worked well and when he was given good support by his allies.

Rommel mainly relied on cooperation with and challenging the Italian high command. Firstly, he was working on the direction of their strategic goals being the same as his, promoting a collective approach for the North African campaign. Furthermore he expressed often his disapproval of the Italians and their effect on the success of operations. Rommel's skilful mastering of this conflicted equation and realizing his targets in spite of the difficulties was a proof of his project management skills and comprehension of global strategy.

A well-known instance in which Rommel backed the Italians was during the Siege of Tobruk. Understanding the strategic utility of the Italian forces in the maintaining of the siege, Rommel backed them directly and also launched coordinated attacks to reinvigorate their resolve and efforts. The leader not only took such chances in the combat zone but he also entered the battle with his friends from Italy to share the burden of combat with them. Thus he has fordtified the Italians and consequently they have done well. Besides, the land-stock among the German and Italian forces was even more consolidated as a result of this

Among his troop's admiration and loyalty, Rommel was able to captivate not only his soldiers but the Italian soldiers under his command as well. In fact, his charisma gained from the charismatic leadership and the leadership to the frontline won the Italian soldiers. Indeed, the Italians' recognition and assessment of their input and steeling of their morale by Rommel's recognition of the entire new troops palyed a bigger role here. No wonder why such a team has been doing excellently in North Africa.

Throughout the North African campaign, Rommel's cooperation with his Italian allies and hence his role as a leader took on a complicated nature that greatly impacted his operations and the successful outcome of the entire campaign. His capacity to manage these relationships and keep the Axis troops united and having a common target was a decisive factor in the good start of his operation. The difficulties he had to go through in making the Italian unit and [this has to stay as is] it's] important to see the necessity of coalition warfare and thus the importance of effective collaboration and coordination among the allied forces.

Rommel's time in North Africa made it very apparent that coalition management was a bigger strategic problem that could not easily be dodged. Managing such diverse forces, all with different abilities and goals, was a major issue for the coalition. Rommel's talents in this line, thus, provided us with the necessary capabilities to not only overcome challenges but also to keep the group cohesive and maintain the effectiveness of the Axis forces. The lessons drawn from Rommel's dealings with the Italians are still of value in the modern coalition war context where the aims and objectives of the allied members must be coherently synchronized to ensure overall success.

When thinking of Rommel's dealings with his Italian General, it is obvious that his diplomatic and leadership skills were the main elements in the whole situation of Axis command in Africa. His initiatives towards the Italian forces and his keenness to drive integration enabled him to cope with the challenging and strained conditions, thus ensuring the operational efficiency of the Axis combined units. Rommel's charisma and his skill to build up a conducive atmosphere for the cooperation among the allies are the reasons for which his name is etched in history as one of the most respected military leaders of World War II.

Strategic Mastery: Rommel's Leadership in North Africa

An intricate analysis of Erwin Rommel's strategies for introducing new supplies and solving the logistical problems that he encountered when fighting in the North African deserts carries the chapter on strategic issues and administrative ingenuity. Despite the hard times he faced, the field was his ground to display unique aptitudes such as dealing with supply problems, using his creativity in desert warfare, as well as regulating the hairy issues between Italy and Rommel himself. Those pieces are the music that his ability to affect the balance and settle the conflicts kept of his capabilities and the solidness of his reputation are confirmed as the "Desert Fox," this being the most famous military leader of World War II.

The provision and management of the supply line were the main logistic and strategic challenges Rommel faced in the North African deserts which were not encountered with any other of his campaigns. They are the troubles of huge spaces and even less favorable environmental conditions meant that the effort to chain a continuous necessary supplies movement makes for a very big task. Besides, the supply routes from Libyan bases were full of risks and thus were periodically attacked by Allied air and naval forces. Rommel's obedience to these constraints and his clever way with captured Allied stores, however, reduced some of the problems with logistics. Nevertheless, supply was from the very beginning the toughest problem with which he had to fight. The underdevelopment of the infrastructure in the region further deepened the hassles thus challenging tireless transport of fuel, ammunition, food, and water.

Rommel's way of fighting the desert wars turned the tide of advanced and early victories. He effectively appropriated the benefits of the blitzkrieg approach to warfare, which meant movements of high speed and attack at the most unexpected time, which after it happened disoriented and outflanked the adversary. By stressing on speed and mobility, he empowered his forces to outflank and maneuver themselves, a thing which the foe fought to do this because of their static and slow motion issues; by this, he would occupy the key areas and crash their defensive plans. Downright genius of Rommel was the fact that he was the fastest, and the enemy was always on the backfoot, which, to his credit, reveals the desert as his domination.

Also, Rommel was a vanguard of the employment of combined arms tactics in the desert. He drew in the infantry, tanks, artillery, and aviation to form a closely joined and modifiable fighting force. Through his innovative approach, Rommel was therefore able to exert pressure from different sides at the same time, hence keeping the enemy from concentrating their defences. The fact that he was able to manage to these muyltiple fronts at the same time is a combination of his foresight as a good tactician and his capability of leading. This kind of practice of war with the desert as a special case was his successful way of making changes and introducing new strategies.

One of the most important aspects of Rommel's leadership was the connections he made with his Italian allies. The Axis powers in North Africa were composed of both German and Italian forces and their collaboration was the key to successful operations. However, the relations between Rommel and the Italian commanders were often in the situation that the Italian forces were less equipped and well-trained than their German counterparts. The main problem that Rommel often faced was that the Italian units were not productive and were not reliable, which resulted in him believing that they were useless.

Notwithstanding the many trials, Rommel realized the significance of keeping a united front and thus conscientiously worked on the improvement of cooperation and teamwork with his Italian allies. His diplomatic competence and his ability to give motivation and inspire loyalty were among the many things that he did for the relationship management. Rommel did not hesitate to take personal risks to protect Italian combat groups. An element of comradeship definitely came from his readiness to endure whatever difficulties were facing the soldiers, and because of it he commanded the respect and loyalty of a lot of Italian soldiers. His Co-operation and mutual support-building were leading factors in the maintenance of the general cohesion and effectiveness of the Axis forces in North Africa.

Rommel's relationship with the Italian high command was a combination of collaboration and confrontation. The somewhat dissimilar strategic objectives and operating methods of the German and Italian command structures, often, led to disputes. Rommel's leadership approach was firm and was to bypass the conservative and slow chains of command, when it is needed, it made the same higher. Nonetheless, his ability in tackling these intricate relationships and realizing his strategies regardless of the numerous problems he faced endorsed the fact that he was an impeccable manager and had far sightedness.

A detailed description of strategic challenges and administrative acumen reveals the wide scope of Rommel's leadership. His performance in dealing with the problems related to logistics and supplies in the hostile desert environment was absolutely crucial to his campaigns. The ways he introduced used desert warfare, especially, his ability to conduct mobile warfare and combined arms tactics, clearly proved him to be tenacious and adaptable. Additionally, his management of the Italian forces with a view to their integration into his forces demonstrated his excellent diplomacy as well as his integrity in setting up a strong and loyal fighting force.

Rommel's offensives in North Africa, in spite of the insurmountable difficulties he encountered, were vivid proof of his knack for coordination and management. His dexterity in the execution of swift, shrewd tactical moves and his relentless pursuit of the strategic goals awarded him the undying label "Desert Fox" and thus, cemented his legacy as a respectful caliber amongst the most talented military commanders during World War II. The wisdom acquired from his North African campaigns, is still being studied and appreciated, as they provide an in-depth perspective into the intricate nature of modern warfare.

His strategic and administrative skills were necessary to his victory as expressed in the experience of Rommel in the Middle East during World War II. His novel innovation in desert fighting, his capacity for handling complicated interalliance cooperation, and his constant drive for operational perfection were all pivotal factors that framed him as a legend. With his status as the "Desert Fox", Rommel proved that he was a model military leader who used the art of war in a smart way; and his work still has a great influence to this day.

Chapter 7

Relationship with Hitler and Nazi Leadership

Rising Star: Rommel's Early Relationship with Hitler

Rommel started to rise in the initial years of his military life whereas, at the same time, the one time victor of El Alamein admirably gained Adolf Hitler's and the Nazi top command's confidence. This time was also the central period, which could be marked as the military high steps of German's Rommel in the heirarchy which were his tactical and productive successes during the French campaign made Hitler interested in him. Hitler being impressed by Rommel's impudence and first-hand victories, which in turn, gave him that the latter was a rising star, having embodied the first and main principle of Blitzkrieg warfare tactic and this styling that will be the motors of German's victory in World War II which was going to take place.

The play was a meteoric climb for Rommel. The successful invasion of France was his first remarkable achievement which led to his rapid progress only in one year, i.e. from distinction to endorsement. Being the commander of the 7th Panzer Division, Rommel showed the innate skill of his to maneuver and outfight the enemies. The were normally, on the other hand, called the "Ghost Division" and for the reason of their rapid and unpredictable movements, and were playing a significant part in the German breakthrough on the Ardennes front and into France. Rommel's tactical use of combined arms, meaning that tanks, troops, and air support were aptly and innovatively brought together, led not only to the breaking of the enemies but also to the acquiring of significant targets.

Hitler, who constantly kept track of the campaign's progress, was much amazed by Rommel's success. Rommel's combat style, comprising such features as his presence in the foremost line and his inspiration methods, was correlated with Hitler's revolutionary understanding of a new type of warfare. The Blitzkrieg virtual weapon, the most important of which was speed, deception, and the carrying out of coordinated attacks, was the idea that Rommel used to create his success. Even the accessibility of strategic goals served for the mutual admiration of Hitler and Rommel.

The rapport between Rommel and Hitler started as a mutual respect and common strategic objectives for the two. Hitler looked at Rommel as a general who could lead his big strategy of swift military force on the ground in a victorious manner. Rommel's popularity in France earned him immediate promotions and high-ranked assignments among them his position to command the Afrika Korps in North Africa. This post was an obvious clue to the strong trust on Rommel by the leader, as he was given the task of commanding such crucial territory in the war.

Rommel's personal relation to Hitler was additionally promoted by the Nazi propaganda machine. Joseph Goebbels, the Propaganda Minister, found in Rommel the best man to make the invincible German warrior image be more common. The stories of Rommel were widely described, and he was personified as a hero in the Hitler epoch. This image did not just bring up Rommel's strength as a soldier but is also gaining him the love of the German people. The claims that Rommel was unbeaten with the armor and added to his reputation and what is more Hitler's confidence in him gained sealization through these propaganda efforts.

"This relationship was indeed a booster for Rommel's career. The backing and support from Hitler was adding new resources and political capital and that was essential for the realization of his war plans. Rommel's demands for a rare platoon and supply were generally addressed by the high administration as an expression of their succincity. It was allowed by this treatment that Rommel became actively involved in the battlefield and sardonosted his opponents not only in the early stages of the North African campaign but also in other instances".

Rommel's post to lead the Afrika Korps in early 1941 stimulated a new relationship tone towards him by Hitler. In the Northern Africa, it was a difficult theatre that was defined by the extreme weather conditions and the intertwined problems with the supply train. Hitler's decision to have Rommel send to that front was purely a sign of his belief in Rommel's abilities. The early successes of Rommel in the desert, including the quick advance into Cyrenaica and the Siege of Tobruk not only to showed him of trust in him also they were things that the Hitler's trust had a value for, they also a word of affirmation.

However, the mutual interactions between Rommel and Hitler were of course not fundamentally melon-flavored there existed a darker side. While Hitler admired Rommel's military expertise and energetic approach to leadership, there were some imperceptible cracks in the friendship that were to be discovered later. Rommel's war solution strategy was essentially manifested in his usage of a tactical retreat when the circumstances dictated a gesture to manage his forces better and this might have been the cause of the disagreement since Hitler was not a very movable person there. These disagreements in the tactics, although not at the outset, ultimately led to the rift between Rommel and Hitler.

Notwithstanding these precursor tensions, the early stage of the Rommel-Hitler pairing featured a target-oriented and rapportful relationship. Rommel's aniggeticsa, dashing, and strict style of fighting the battles that Hitler wanted was what made Hitler himself prompt a vision of a less trustworthy and an indefeasible German nation. The moral and trusting supplied to Rommel from the Hitler not only allowed him to launch his aggressive and fresh tricks but also assisted him in leading and valuing his early victories that would eventually become associated with him as a commander and one of the most skillful German ones.

Rommel succeeded not only in his dynamic leading but also with his inspiring his soldiers with strong self-confidence and loyalty. His position as a frontliner and his participation in the daily life of his men and the attitudes of his troops showing him were the respect and admiration of them, which never were in short supply, his presence being the principal reason for that. Apart from his glorious leadership style, Rommel's strategic genius was favorable to his being a leader in the military and a weapon of high value for--as-a ruler in the war.

With the outset of the relationship between Hitler and Rommel, it was characterized by the two parties' appreciation to each other and the hope to-achieve a military success. Rommel's meteoric rise to the top of the German military was the result of Hitler's support that made him realize his tricky plans as well as win a few battles. But on the other hand, the difficulty of their relations with the passage of time--and the disagreements in strategy that followed suggested that there were some obstacles to come. Inasmuch as they might be a bone of contention later, the service and belief of Rommel's and Hitler's towards that affected the former so much that he became what he is now–the "Desert Fox."

Clash of Strategies: Rommel and Hitler's Diverging Visions

In spite of the steady and solid support and trust that characterized Erwin Rommel's relationship with Adolf Hitler and the Nazi leadership, strategic disagreements soon began to emerge, which made their once strong alliance gradually unsteadier. Rommel's practical and versatile battle ideas usually collided with Hitler's operations, which used more rigid and ideologically driven strategies. These differences in military philosophy became very prominent as the war progressed. Indeed, the Tactical Byzantine-style Differentiation of the North African front, where that of Rommel was down on terra firma and at times ran counter to the former's ethnocentric aerial bombing dream, was one of the key areas of discrepancies.

One of the main points of debate, among other things, between Rommel and Hitler was the former's contention to stop at all costs to the latter. Hitler's strategic viewpoint was significantly overshadowed by his belief that the territorial or hidden significance of the symbolic or psychological aspects of it was preeminent. The idea that led him to introduce the following as a matter of fact that - German forces must not to leave their positions at the last man even it will be a case of defeat by enemy advances. Rommel, however, was aware of the importance of tactical withdrawals to keep his forces strong for future battles. He was of the opinion that retreating from time to time to gather the needed forces or reload and then conduct a strong attack at a later time was needed.

The North African campaign was the best example of the strategic gaps between them. The link between Rommel's victory in this arena and his grace in rapid, mobile operations, which were suitable for the desert environment, cannot be stressed more. The vast and open plains of North Africa required a high degree of adaptability over a large area of movement, and Rommel was always there. However, the relief and resupplying of combatants - or staying back to defend freely, unlike the plain- was not the only thing getting in the way; these also hampered the whole campaign.

Rommel was mostly in conflict with Hitler and the OKW (Oberkommando der Wehrmacht) over the war's plan in North Africa. While Rommel was arguing for a strategy that would allow fast changes and retreats when needed, Hitler insisted on military fortifications and unstoppable military operations. With this strict attitude, Hitler and his subordinates often did not take into account the realities on the field, so under such circumstances, they often put Rommel's troops in really difficult positions.

The Battle of El Alamein overlaid in 1942 showed the bad outcomes of these strategic differences. Despite Rommel's first progress and appealing the Fuhrer for backup and resupply, the fatal orders from Berlin forced him to break the defense that was not possible due to the lack of supplies. The obstinacy to retain the ground without adequate backing resulted in heavy losses and a forced departure. Rommel's exasperation with these decisions was made worse when he witnessed firsthand that Hitler's consistent strategies were indeed getting it wrong at the operational level of his forces.

Rommel's disillusionment with the Nazi leaders' strategic decisions was not limited to the tactical conflicts only, but also to the ideological matters. He was voicing out the urgency for a pragmatic, and flexible view on war since the situation was changing rapidly, especially with the Allies overpowering. Rommel's knowledge of the strategic picture and his realistic estimate of the situation are what distinguished him as a chief deepley conscious of the fact that the German warfare had certain limits and vulnerabilities.

The root of this motivation to challenge Hitler's orders, which though was derived from the dedication to the army's performance, yet it strained the relationship between Rommel and the Nazi leadership. Hitler, who was of the opinion that loyalty and obedience were the most important characteristics of a person, saw Rommel's critics of him as a threat to his authority. The trust broken between the two of them was further reinforced by Rommel's critique of the tasks and problems posed on him and his groups. His loud argument that the best way to generate a strategic plan is by having more room for change was thought of as disobedience. It made Hitler and Rommel's relationship worse.

Rommel's dissension was also based on his observations of the general course of the war. He was against the failure of the Nazi leadership to solve the problems of the supply chain and to foresee the difficulties in raising the force of German soldiers. Rommel knew that without a strog and a very reliable supply chain the grand strategies programmed by Hitler were in vain. His talking about the logistics of support and the making of a reasonable plan, on the other hand, underlined one of the fundamental differences that occured between the field commanders and the government.

The difference in their perspectives on military strategy was shaped largely by the dissimilarities in their intuitions of the military strategy. Rommel's approach was mainly adapted to the science of war, focusing on the changeability, flexibleness, and the most efficient use of the available resources. However, Hitler's tactical plans were spontaneously chosen by ideological viewpoints or personal interest in acquiring major victories. His lack of adaptative thinking prevente him from devising a more practical and effective response to the war issues that were arising at the moment.

Rommel's strategic conflicts with Hitler fundamentally affected his career and the broader management of the war. His impetus to push for a more practical and flexible military plan, despite the unfavorable personal and professional repercussions, indicated his devotion to military effectiveness. Still, it also had him in opposition to a higher-up hierarchy that was more concerned with conceptual purity than practicality.

The Rommel-Hitler conflict of paths is a prime example of the schism in the German military command during the Second World War. It highlights the dilemma of military leaders who were torn between the demands of their political superiors and the ground-level realities of their operations. The story of Rommel's challenges provides the prime example of the linkage between strategic errors and the complicated web of local politics and military.""

The Rommel-Hitler strategic clashes compel a reflection that rigid and ideological paths are not a one-size-fits-all strategy in military conflict rather they conduct a limitation. It underlines the importance of agility, adaptability and pragmatic decision making in the achievement of operational goals. Rommel's reputation as a military leader is not solely based on his tactical expertise but also on his principled commitment to the creation of practical and realistic military plans even if it comes with a heavy fight from the highest command.

Rommel and the July 20 Plot: The Plot Against Hitler

The rampant progress of World War II and the no-win position of Germany bred discontent among Erwin Rommel towards Adolf Hitler and Nazi political leaders. At this point, he had become so alienated from the movement that he sanctioned the July 20th conspiracy. It was a pretty audacious play but it was the last straw in the play of the plotters who were against Hitler and tried to reinstate the old regime by any means necessary. There seems to be no consensus on the role that Rommel played in this affair and that leaves this historical argument unresolved if he was just an accomplished supporter of the dissidents or yet more disgusted with Adolf's governance.

The July 20th matter was orchestrated by people who were convinced that the only salvation of Germany would be his removal successfully or else such a fate, as had befallen all other countries to which he had lost would abide the country. To kill Hitler, the plotters intended to take over the government and thus be available for peace talks with the Allies. The idea was that by the elimination of Hitler they could end up the war before the Germans met their doom and became the victims of all the disastrous concepts.

Rommel entered the formula since he was convinced with his own eyes that there was literally the only thread that covered the end of the war-as quickly as possible. What he underwent and lay bare of the real war plans were enough to prove him wrong about the matter that Hitler at the wheel of a locomotive would lead the way through more chaos yet. Robust Rommel with his loyalty to the soldiers' honor code and his deep and abiding love for his home place saw it as a duty of his to go collaboratively with the rest of the group.

On account of his reputation in the military and his popularity, Rommel persuaded the plotters to trust him. His advanced and particularly disciplined way of handling soldiers and officers made him a perfect candidate for the position of masterminding a conspiracy in the army. People planning the demise of the tyrant thought that Rommel's mere participation would be enough to persuade others as well as making their coup more likely to achieve.

Rommel's involvement in the scheme, nevertheless, was done with great care and without haste. He did not make any efforts to plan or carry out the assassination, probably because of his non-emotional logic and the fact that he clearly saw the high dangers surrounding the bombings. The general had always recognized that any attempt to dethrone Hitler is dangerous, not just to his person, but to the people who are with him. He realized the devastation that met the people who did not go along with it and were the first to gain bile from the Führer in case of a failed coup.

Although Rommel was extremely careful; his affiliation with the plotters was obviously taken as something big as to put him on the list of the suspects after the failed attempt. On July 20, 1944, Colonel Claus von Stauffenberg set off a bomb at the Wolf's Lair in East Prussia, but the bomb that exploded did not end up killing Hitler as it was planned. The plot was exposed in a rapid manner, and a strict policy on the conspirators was carried out. The majority of the discipline was laid, tortured for their involvement and some of them were executed.

The close link Rommel had to the terrible crime caused people to look into his case very intently. In spite the lack of clear data as to his role in planning some phase or other of the attempt itself, his siding with the plotters and his disillusionment with the idea of Hitler were sufficient for the Nazis to take him for an enemy. The Gestapo, the specific secret service unit of the Nazi leader, started probing into Rommel's part, while losing his life was less than possible.

Rommel's fate gave the Nazi leaders a headache. They were caught in a bind, as Rommel's popular support and the publicity associated with his presence in the government could lead to the annulment of the trial and the execution of the whole event. Hitler and his inner circle chose a more discrete method to deal with Rommel. Two generals, on October 14, 1944, made a visit to Rommel's house and gave him an option: he could face a trial in a public place that would result in disgrace and death, or he could instead take his life by giving a promise that his family would not be prosecuted.

There is a right to choices of conflicts. Roman instead chose taking his life because he was in an unbearable situation. Colonel took poison and thus he killed himself. The common explanation to the public for the death of Rommel was that the latter had died from the old wounds he got during an earlier air raid. The state honored him with a military funeral, during which full military honors were bestowed on him, thus the publicity continued to recognize him as a hero of the Third Reich and concealed the real details of his death.

Rommel's journey from being a pro-Hitler and Hitler's right-hand man into the July 20th plot and the forcible death marked a tragic chapter in his military career. His original position as an enthusiastic supporter and confidante of Hitler had turned into possibly the most intense of the instances of his disillusionment and betrayal, it further demonstrated the great impact of strategic and ideological differences on his relationship with the Nazi leadership that he experienced. Rommel's defensibility against Hitler's coercive governance and his ultimate sacrifice delineated the ethical and moral binding faced by the soldiers within the Germany military who were against the Nazi regime.

Rommel's history is not clear because his undertaking tries to prove it. Some consider the German general as the first man to dare to oppose the totalitarian regime. One person, on the other hand, may find it difficult to believe that he was a dedicated member of the plot. Regardless of the actual impact of his engagement, Rommel's rejection of Hitler's power is evident from his participation in the scheme. This rejection was a direct one though it was silent. In fact, it was a manifestation of the military's nobility and ratified the spirit and honor of Rommel in a way. His death is remembered as an example of the severe trials a resistance movement faces in a despotic regime, both collectively and individually. It is hard for me to keep pushing the boys to be the best that they can be when I do not stay true to my word by making my best effort to be the best that I can be. And what is the hardest is when they notice that I'm not keeping my promise or not doing my best. Not because I cannot do it, I have the power to be the best of who I am if I make everything with sincerity and truth.

One of the chapters that World War II would still be incomplete without was the July 20 Plot, which brought to the fore the resistance movement within Germany. The record of Rommel in association with the whole plot introduces both sides of his life: the commander of an African army and a conspirator. This shows him as a person with whom the war choice of the generals would be with or without the tyranny that Hitler is at. Although not from a distance that our parents and grandparents used to witness world war two, we are at a time in our history where the results may be just as devastating as they were both to the soldiers and the civilian population. As age catches up with me I find it is no longer appealing to teach kids how to become best by showing them and telling them when I am not living that out by myself because that on its own fails to convey a compelling message to the students. If you do it sincerely and sincerely, you will definitely become the best of what you are and will be able to overcome any obstacles and challenges that come your way.

The Price of Defiance: Consequences and Downfall

The plot against Hitler was a wicked tragedy for Erwin Rommel, who used to be favored by Adolf Hitler and the Nazi management. It was a brave and desperate suicidal mission to save the second World War, but its failure paved the way for a great number of bloody reprisals. In the wake of these events, the Gestapo carried out an extensive investigation which brought the secret the conspiracy to the surface, the arrest, the torment and the execution of many of the people involved being the result. Rommel, being who he was and the kind of propaganda tool he was for the tyrant regime, at first was able to avoid being captured right away. Nonetheless, his destiny was cemented in a more rotten way.

Even though the relationship that Rommel had with the people who organized the plot was only on the sidelines and he was very careful, it was still like a sign pointing right at him. A deep scrutiny of Gestapo Authority made it clear that Rommel commiserated with the plotters, a matter, which was so significant that the Nazi leadership could not ignore it. Hitler identifying Rommel's iconic cardinality and the ai of his public trial as well as potential backlash offered him a choice (face trial/public and sure execution, or live alone in pain for years and have his family safe). The measure was taken to silence the general leaving him his credit of a hero and thus avoiding the possible negative influence caused by his death.

The diguise was kept by Rommel till the end of his life when he chose to swallow a cyanide pill and slept forever on October 14, 1944. Consequently, it was a terrible suicide of the person who had taken one of Germany's most admired generals. His demise was officially covered by the statement of him being hurt during a deluded time of war, which kept up his good name and loyalty to the ruling authorities. The state funeral was offered to him by the Fourth Reich his body as he was his most preferred son. The spectacular theater was meant to keep from the public what really happened comparing to the true hurtful and calculating nature of Hitler's regime.

Rommel's connection with the July 20 Plot and his subsequent downfall was a very sad and moving end to his career in the military. The initial support and reliance on Hitler that he went through were now expressed in the form of disappointment and disloyalty. That served to point out the intended or even inevitable lack of easy decisions facing Rommel and Hitler. That of course was the discordant relationship and finally, the destructive one between the leader of the country and the main general. In addition to the fact that his military strategies and contributions to the Army were outstanding, the epiphany of Rommel to go against the Hitler was moral and ethical whereby he killed himself, remained one of the main moral and ethical achievements accomplished by those who were within the German military and aimed at the dismantling of the Nazi.

The defeat of Rommel was a real-life example of the inhumanity of the hierarchy within the Nazi regime. The city leaders' ruling with an iron hand on anyone who dared to oppose the regime or voice out their sentiments no matter what their past contributions were is the strongest leniency point of them hence the brutality can be witnessed through the way he was dispatched. The use of psychological manipulation in order to prompt someone to commit suicide and still claiming to be honourable is the sacrifice that Hitler and his powerful group were ready to make in order to protect their power over the nation. The method was very efficient not just for silencing the enemy. It was a necessary precaution measure meant to reach out to any other wavering members in and all the groups.

The very devastating end of Rommel was also to him the multifaceted interaction of personal honour and steadfastness with the viability of political ideas. Rommel's act to shoot himself in his heart in order to protect his relatives was his very last personal sacrifice. Thus, the Holocaust can be shown as the time of many such clashes when the impression of individual freedom is counteracted by the close constraints of both societal and familial conveniences.

Rommel's legacy is complicated and complex despite his death's background. Foremost, he was a military genius and started innovative ways of military operations that have been thoroughly learned and imitated by the military history students. On the other hand, his association with the Nazi regime and the fact that he got involved in the initially failed July 20 coup gives him the figure of a person who understood his duty as a soldier. Nevertheless, he had his personal objection to the cruelty of the regime he was serving that he might have been. The Nazi regime were still capable of catching his attentions with their misuse of power and brutality. His fall from grace serves as a constant reminder of the hidden ethical problems faced by military leaders in the times of war, more so those under very dictatorial regimes. His life is an initial walking of ambition and success, and then, this period is followed by a step-by-step realization of the detours one has to take in moral aspects necessary to keep being successful. Although Rommel's resistance was not the most courageous and did not last too long either, the tragedy he had to endure, in the end, demonstrated how high a price he had to pay for his principled stance.

The results of the July 20 Plot and Rommel's crash serve as a reflection of the larger issues involved in defiance within the system in which there is no tolerance for it. The brute-force that was on display after the assassination attempt, which was not successful, was the system's iron will to maintain power regardless of the cost. The destinies of Rommel and his fellow conspiratorial companions point out the very real dangers that one has to cope with if they wish to be on the side that stands against Hitler as these conditions were some of the hardest encountered in the history.

Rommel's personality is still made known in the story as a strong one despite the ironies in the process whereby the narrative includes the implementation of the brutal force and the malevolent leadership that governed the members. His tragic end and the brilliancy in other military fields issue a clear and provoking example of the moral and personal questions that need to be solved by those who refuse to join the ranks of the tyrants. In the quest for justice, Rommel's life is continually under the microscope of scrutiny as his reign and perishing are indeed the clear groundward study of values, duty, and resistance in the most terrible periods of humankind.

Rommel and Hitler: A Tale of Loyalty, Disillusionment, and Defiance

The part on Erwin Rommel's relationship with Adolf Hitler and the Nazi ruling regime describes the process of his contacts with the authorities of the state, from the first support and mutual respect to the strategic discussions and the participation in the July 20 coup. This career path shows the differences in Rommel's career and how strategy and ideology changed his role in the Nazi country. His being in a very difficult situation, he didn't live long, but being the "Desert Fox" and one of World War II's most reputable military players was himself, therefore, the proof of loyalty, duty and moral conviction in the time of war are very complicated issues.

Rommel and Hitler's relationship in the beginning was a combination of equal respect and common goals. Hitler was stimulated by Rommel's tactical flair during the French campaign and he looked at him as a new star in the skies of the German army. Rommel's meteoric rise to the top and his high-level assignments, for example, his command of the Afrika Korps, were a clear indication of the trust Hitler had in him. The time of support was especially favorable for his career since he had the means and support to execute his military campaigns as the resources and the political power needed for his ambitious military campaigns were provided to him.

Nevertheless, as the war went on, there occurred some strategic discrepancies on the grounds, which corroded the ties of Rommel to the Nazi regime. Rommel's flexible approach to warfare with regard to Hitler's rigid and ideologically driven strategies was the primary cause of the dispute. One of the highly disputable matters between the two was the steadfastness of Hitler who never wanted to give up an inch of ground whatever the cost, which was in complete contrast to Rommel who thought that tactical withdrawals were essential for the conservation of his forces for the next battles. Especially during the North African campaign, the latter was not the case as Rommel was suggested the best option. He was the advocate of the mobile method, as the best instrument for matching the ever-changing battlefield. In the case of Hitler, the picture of the ideal solution was the static and offensive operations, often emphasizing the latter, which occurred regardless of the logistical and tactical necessities on the ground.

Rommel's frustration with the strategic decisions made over the times increased. He voiced his growing dissatisfaction at the unrealistic and inflexible policies of the war, mainly after the change of the war tide began to swing the way of the Allied Powers. His flexibility on Hitler's commands, even though it was something he insisted would lead to the efficiency of the military, was the main issue which started threatening their relationship and reducing almost zero trust among them.

The mounting disappointment finally completed with Rommel's taking part in the conspiracy, an assassination attempt on Hitler, and a downfall of the Nazis.CH[1] However, despite certain questions from historians regarding the exact nature of his involvement in the plot, it is obvious that he was at least for the plotters and let down with Hitler's governorship. The participants, a group of German high-ranking army men and ordinary people who wanted to have Hitler out of the way and make a peace deal with the Allies, had put in place this scheme. Rommel's cooperation was based on his belief that Germany's only chance to live was to stop the war before the complete triumph.

Rommel's role was, in the first place, conservative; he did not take a direct part in the planning, or even the execution, which is likely connected to his being a realist and the fact the danger was high. Despite that, the connections he had with the conspirators gave grounds for the liberation of the plot. During the Gestapo's search, the conspiracy's details were found out, and Rommel was the one who was to be suspected of sympathies, after which Hitler gave him a choice between a trial and the inevitable debasement and execution or his family would be spared if he committed suicide. As per Rommel's decision, on Oct 14, 1944, he made use of cyanide to kill himself privately in order to save his family from public humiliation.

Rommel's career in the military ended tragically, marking the final chapter of his otherwise impeccable career. Starting off with full support and trust from Hitler, he had turned into disillusionment and betrayal, which have shown the relationship between Rommel and the Nazi leaders, which was complex and ultimately very injurious. Nevertheless, Rommel, a man renowned not only for his strategic brilliance and for the crucial part he played in the military effort, was resolute and adhered to his ethical principles. This has emphasized the ethical and moral concerns that the German High-Ranking Members of the military opposed the Nazi regime ghazwa within Germany.

Rommel's portrayal as the "Desert Fox" signifies his competency as a military leader and the integrity he demonstrated amidst a tyrant rule. His track from being in the high trust of his superiors to become a traitor who has seen the deep impact of tactics and ideology on his career graph. His connection with Hitler and its developments give a different angle on the matter of honesty, compliance and the personal declaration among nations, at times of war. Rommel's journey is indicative of the internal and moral struggles the people who take a stand against oppressive regimes go through and this can be even at the cost of their own life is a valuable lesson to his story.

Rommel's biography and vocation are lauded and studied by young people who look up to them for teachings on good leadership and stratagem as well as the human capacity for resilience and moral integrity. His argument to the authority and his final and ultimate tactic show the ongoing importance of ethics mainly in particular dangerous times. Whether history will judge him as positively or negatively, Rommel still remains a dynamic symbol of tension between duty, dignity, and resistance always reminding us of our need for justice and humanity in the face of adversity.

Chapter 8

Final Campaigns and Last Days

Fortifying the Atlantic: Rommel's Last Stand on the Western Front

At the end of 1943, Rommel was given a job as the leader of Armed Group B, which he was to assess and intensify the Atlantic Wall, a chain of the great number of very strong and closely joined together against an enemy lines that was this intended to make it difficult for the enemy. to make an enemy invasion. This was a very important military decision, since the Western Front was starting to be viewed with greater and greater probability as a primary target for a major Allied assault. Always the one who found practical ways out of them and acted in an efficient manner, Rommel approached the new and formidable problem with the same might and insight that he had showed earlier on.

While going through the Wall's placement, Rommel was 1000 the rate of threats worried because of the worse condition. In the face of the supposed impregnability of the site, Rommel soon discovered the truth of the matter, that it was just Nazi propaganda that exaggerated the mighty of the Atlantic Wall. Indeed, this wall, though numerous in some areas, was either incomplete or irregular along the whole shore. Most of the defensive positions were not suitable for assault by modern tactics and did not have the capabilities to send off well-armed and well-prepared invaders.

His foremost concern was the correction of the deficiencies, start the construction of beach fortifications, and then make sure to do it by his favoring and guiding-slowing the opposing forces. He recognized that the first obstacle to be overcome for the defense of the strategy was to slow down and destroy the enemy before he gained a foothold. In this regard, he did that with the placement of obstacles that could destroy tanks, which were Czech hedgehogs, Rommel's Asparagus, which were mines set up. near wooden stakes, and allies would enter the beaches with which the incoming enemy troops could land. created the problems that the weapons firing through the layers of defense than the enemy shall easily be destroyed.

Rommel, on top of the physical obstacles, highlights the minefield as the most important one. He commanded that millions of mines be distributed over the beaches and in shallow areas, which should multiply the number of different threats and also make them less predictable as to where they might be. As a result, the landmines were only set to steer enemies into kill zones, the very places with the best visibility for inward-bound projectiles. The point was to utilise the placements of these minefields laterally across other fortifications for the most effective blockade and cohesion.

Fortified gun emplacements that were reinforced were another major component of Rommel's defensive plan. He was aware of the fact that the stationary attacking spots have to be covered by compactly positioned, well-secured positions to assure that concurrent attack of more ships are impeded. The emplacements were built with some extra strong concrete that could be bombarded and could even come with artillery of great weight or anti-tank guns and machine guns. To defend themselves against enemy aircraft, Rommel also encouraged installing anti-aircraft weapons. These points were fortified to grant uninterrupted and concentrated fire, which would abort the landing and do damage to them.

Despite the overwhelming significance of fortifications, it was evident that Rommel knew that fortitude alone was not sufficient in resisting a diverse enemy. To the end that the dynamic barriers would be capable of standing up to the potential invasion by a stronger and more resourceful enemy, he insisted on the introduction of mobile reserves. The use of wheeled and tracked motorised vehicles allowed Rommel to place tanks, mechanised infantry vehicles in key areas in his defense line to be used in case the Allies tried to breach. He believed that overpowering the invasion lay in the ability to carry out rapid and decisive counterattacks, thereby, forbidding the soldiers to consolidate their landing points and, thus, make the landing inland.

Rommel's lead in the reinforcement of the Atlantic Wall manifested his broad comprehension of fast-paced warfare and the vitality of adjusting to the new environment. He was fully aware of the insufficiency of the traditional static defences in an era of rapid mechanized warfare and air superiority. He came up with a conflicting strategy that aimed to create a defence system with flexible and mobile response forces combined with fixed fortifications. The plan's approach was on the one hand, exploiting the defender's innate advantage of a statically secured location and at the same time, mitigating the weaknesses brought forward by the new form of warfare.

Determining the sentiments of the drawback, however, he still had to make the brave journey of his thought process still sticking to the Computer memory and focusing the heavy metal of the frontline. Resources were rare and the Munich Pact with the Soviet Union that was required almost all of Germany's manpower on the Eastern Front was another failure on the part of the Nazis. Despite this, Rommel faced a number of other difficulties such as overcoming the resistance of an entrenched bureaucracy and the divergent demands of colleagues at the Nazi regime. His nonstop pressure on the procurement of the required personnel and materials were his response to the evidence that the western conflict will determine the line between winning and losing.

Rommel's prelude to the Atlantic Wall was a reflection of his bigger military strategic approach as well. He was deeply convinced of the advantages of flexibility, adaptability, and provision of active defense. Giving the paramount importance to rapid response and tightly integrated defense was his way of showing his ability to think even more innovative and foresaw the way warfare might change. Rommel's Atlantic Wall strategy was more complex than the mere construction of defense facilities. Standing as one, it was about transmitting dynamic and flexible defensive system power strong enough for the full Allied onslaught to be overcome.

The Atlantic Wall, reinterpreted by Rommel, bears witness to his strategic foresight and military acumen. Because the fortifications and preparations he suggested could not actually hinder the success of the D-Day landings, they made operations for the Allied forces much tougher and long-drawn-out. Rommel's contribution to the fortification activities made manifest his unwaveringly dutiful character and his unstoppable eagerness to war mastery.

Rommel's command in Brittany was a multilateral one. The effectiveness of fortification on the Atlantic Wall indicated his ability to adjust to new strategic demands and his grasp of the multifaceted nature of modern warfare. Though the ultimate inability to hold off the enemy was mainly due to multiple factors that were out of his control, Yet, Rommel's strategic intuition and his resoluteness to defend Germany to the extreme showed his undying loyalty for his country and his soldiers. His tenure as commander of Army Group B remains one of the decisive chapters in his military career, disclosing both his qualities as a commander and the considerable obstacles he had to face in the final years of the war.

The Storm Breaks: Rommel and the Normandy Invasion

The Atlantic Wall, a system of defensive fortifications stretching along the French coast from Belgium to Spain, in the hands of the Germans, was supposed to be impermeable. However, the invasion of Normandy on 6 April 1944 was a turning point in World War II. D-Day was the day on which Allied forces launched a major and unified attack on the beaches of Normandy under the codename Operation Overlord and thus were able to sweep away German defenses, which were caught unawares. General Rommel, who knew that the Allies might invade in Normandy, was not at his post when the invasion happened as he was with his family in Germany at the time. The element of surprise and the sheer scale of the invasion were both so big that the German soldiers had a hard time defending themselves. This eventually had the most detrimental impact on Western Europe.

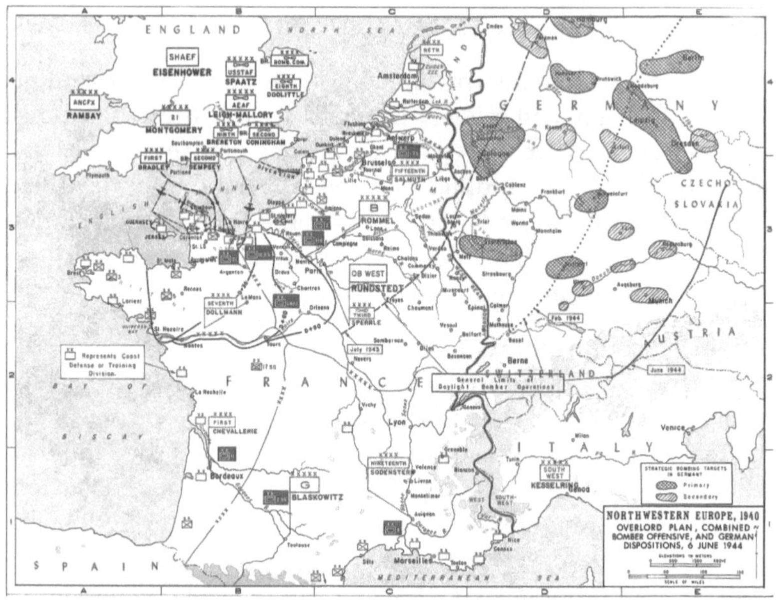

Operation Overlord was not only the result of careful and detailed planning but also the product of the collaborative efforts of the Allies. The Allied invasion troops, including US, UK, Canada, and other nations' forces, together with the navy and air force, conducted a strong offensive against the German military. On the morning of June 6, 1944, the soldiers and military equipment on top of the warships set out to Utah, Omaha, Gold, Juno, and Sword, respectively, and they were among the main targets for the aircraft and battleships. Even Rommel's many warnings and the fact that he had already taken some initial measures as a warning were not enough, and the defenders were still caught off their guard.

He has always always demanding of a very energetic response and immediate measures-supposed to be taken in case of any potential enemy landing. By using a strategy of quickly regaining the lost ground in the areas where they attacked while driving the enemy at the same time, he was convinced that the greatest chance of defeating the invasion lay in the approach. However, at the crucial moment of the invasion, his absence made the situation more complicated than it should have been. The initial disorder and the fact that the German troops could not act according to a single command were the most important things that allowed the Allies to establish a foothold on the beaches, thus enabling them to further advance inland.

Hearing about the invasion, Rommel speedily returned to the front to plan a counterattack and rescue the Allied advance. His coming back as commander was marked by urgency as well as despair. Rommel got it that the victorious invasion hinged on the speed and effectiveness of the German troops' counteroffensive. He regrouped the forces and ordered several counterattacks to get rid of the Allied beachheads. He worked hard but all his efforts were weakened by some essential reasons.

Among the greatest problems Rommel could face, the air superiority of the Allies was the most difficult to surmount. The skies over Normandy were full of Allied aircraft which performed close air support to the forces on the ground and picked out German reinforcements and supply lines. This air predominance was the major force that paralyzed German troops and did not allow them to equip themselves with the weapon and mission very well, so they had to come up with the organization and execution of the counterattacks. The never-ending danger of air strikes forced Rommel's troops to make their movements undercover and limited their capacity to respond quickly and flexibly to the new on-the-ground situation.

Along with the Allied naval attack, the invasion was the first and most prominent assistant. The very heavy naval guns were able to effectively neutralize German positions by striking their defenses and causing many casualties. The naval aid made the allies move farther and brought a constant flow of reinforcements and supplies, thus strengthening their forces. The joint action of the air and naval fleets produced a shield too strong for Rommel's units to break.

By a lack of agreement and the fact that the German command was quite decentralized, the defense strategy as proposed by Rommel was ceased. Rommel advocated for the concentration of armoured reserves close to the coast to increase rapid counterattacks. Other people in the German command structure, including Field Marshal Gerd von Rundstedt, however, favored a more dispersed deployment of forces. This strategic disagreement led to delays and lack of cohesion in the German response. The slow speed of mobilizing the Panzer divisions, of which Rommel had planned to use for quick counterattacks, led to the Allies' ability to concentrate their positions and advance further inland.

It was certainly no easy feat for the Allies to overcome such mighty barriers, still Rommel's well-known toughness and tactical skill in holding the Allied advance showed. He supervised some counteroffensive operations himself and made some changes to the battlefield in an effort to slow the advancing Allies. However, the enormous number of Allied forces and the constant bitter backing from them became a task too demanding. The Allies' capability for continuous and coordinated attacks gradually destroyed the German defenses.

The Allies' success in Normandy was the first step in the defeat of the German forces in the Western Europe. The taking of the beachheads allowed for the force buildup and the next offensives that took place eventually led to the liberation of France and the advance into Germany. Rommel's failure to push back the invasion despite his farsightedness and efforts, portrayed the overwhelming logistic and tactical support for the Allies.

The part of the battle of Normandy that Rommel played was quite remarkable on the one side for his great potential as a military leader while on the other side the impossibility of the conditions faced by him. His ability to foresee the invasion and his indefatigable efforts of defense against it only affirmed his strategic sagacity. However, the impossibility of establishing any defense line against the overwhelming Allied air and naval power, the disagreements among managers of their respective defenses, and the apparent size of the operation, which was too big to be applied, made the objectives he pursued zero out.

The Normandy operation was the best proof of the Allies burst of planning expertise, outdoing logistical supply, and closer coordination. It also brought about a sea change in the rhythm of the war, and the Allied forces clearly took the active side in the game. For Rommel, it was a very irritating moment confirming the idea that Germany is going to lose. The explanation of his next moves and his decisions is that he saw the war already turning against Germany and reacted under that awareness.

Normandy, the First of June will continue to be the most shining example of military strategy in history, and Rommel's participation, although it was not successful at the end, is an indispensable part of this story. His military tips and the complex problems with which he was struggling contribute to our understanding of the intricacies of the skills of command and the inordinate influence of the overall strategic and logistic factors on the outcomes of military operations. Rommel's ineffective operations in Normandy show that in the history of the conflict, his was that of a very strong military technician who fought hard and smartly in spite of his weakness and the big advantage of the enemy.

Rommel's Wounding and the Impact on the German War Effort

On July 17, 1944, Erwin Rommel, one of the most famous and loved military commanders of Germany, was badly hurt in Normandy, which was a big deal for him, and the German war effort also changed. He was hit by a very vulnerable gun and as a result he had to be put away from the active army for weeks. The event happened during his drive on an open staff car right at the front lines, where suddenly, a plane hit him. The pilot decided to hit Rommel's vehicle, and he suffered numerous fractures of his skull and facial injuries that were so grave even if his withdrawal was involuntary.

The wounds Rommel had were very sensitive to the German army in more than one way, both of them were symbolic and severity was connected to it. Rommel, who was most famous for being a great commander and for his innovative fighting strategy, was a key factor in the defense of Germany's D-Day against the Allied force. His image at the front was a strong, positivism-intensive source among the German soldiers while his impressive series of moves was crucial to the coordination of the counter-attacks and the building of the fortifications.

At first, things looked like a mess after the attack had occurred. The injured man was speedily transported to a nearby field infirmary, and there, the doctors had to have a look at what injuries he got. The cracked skull could have been fatal, as well as his facial injuries being quite severe while medical treatment was not very easy. The initial results looked bad, and everybody was skeptical about whether Rommel might live through the excruciating treatment. The bomb didn't just make him physically handicapped but also neglected him from the essential command system at a time when his leadership was most sought for.

The process of Rommel's recovery was the opposite of quick, it was full of agony and roughness. His town, Herrlingen, is where he lived and for a few weeks he was there getting better. The level of injury he suffered was so large that this is the first time he has had to face not just the physical impacts, which were immense, but also the mental ones.

Rommel was closely experiencing the rapidly changing situation on all fronts and was thus extremely alarmed. The allied powers succeeded in making considerable progress in Normandy, and the German military was thus unable to put up an effective defense. In light of the added implementations, Rommel had to be away from the field time. Now that the strike of war was at its highest point, his tactical knowledge as well as his inspiration were both absent.

While in recovery, Rommel didn't lose touch with his staff and the high command, but his capacity to make things happen was mostly inert. What he thought about the doomed events in Normandy was the only thing that seemed to be his priority then. The Allies' advance was so rapid and aggressive that the German defenses were just being wasted. There was a feeling that there were just no countermeasures that the German military could find the energy and resources to use efficiently. Rommel still had a strategic head but he was unable to steer the boat because he was laid up with an injury.

This period also provides Rommel with time for him to think of the whole picture of Germany at that time. There is no doubt that the strategic mistakes, the shortage of the railway system, and the internal conflicts of the Third Reich were visible to all. Hitler was a major critic of Rommel's for holding positions that were not well defended, especially when the defense had to be the main priority. What he had seen and reflected on during his recovery only supported this judgment that Germany's war effort was being mishandled at the top levels.

The limitations put on Rommel by the injuries made him very angry. He was personal a man that was always found near the front lines and checked everything with his own eyes. Thus, being kept inside his home was something very strange for him. It was not just tough for Rommel alone, as he felt had fallen notably hard for the German army as well, that time of no functioning was actually both a personal struggle for Rommel and his fading away for the German army. His infusion of enthusiasm and leadership into the troops was indeed on the material, and the troops he inspired had already loyally come to depend on him. The gap left by his missing out, and the contributors who took over his place have to deal with the difficulties of the military in leadership and motivation.

The wounds that Rommel suffered and the healing process that followed brought about negative results in the German military operation. The empty space left by his non-presence vividly demonstrated the troubles of the German military in terms of leadership and morale. There was no one else who could come up with the same set of tactics, dialogue persuasions, and strategies, which would produce the desired results. The substitutes who came to govern the role after him did not possess the influence and skills of Rommel, bringing more problems to the generals on the front line.

Rommel did not have a very good time when he was making every effort to regain his health. The enemy used the German military's disarray to expand their military operations and took long strides into the occupied territory that they planned. The absence of

Rommel in action in this particular stage was a harbinger of the impasse on the part of the Allies and allowed them to thrust ahead.

Rommel's mental state was not the only thing that was hit by his hell-wound. The German military and people all over the country were startled by the event. Rommel was a symbol of German resistance as well as military power and his disabilities portrayed the Third Reich's unstable standing more dramatically. Propaganda that formerly was painting Rommel as an unconquerable hero was heaping contempt on their own reality.

The eventual return of Rommel to his active service again was not important; the true change of dynamics was caused by the speed with which the war was developing. He did recover the wound enough to get involved again to some extent, but the situation was so critical that he could't do that to the extent when his suggestions were taken into consideration but nonetheless he remained a potentially fundamental figure.

Rommel's wound and recovery are the specific examples of the widespread plight of the German army in the last days of World War II. In reality, the fortitude of leaders was in high demand and the devastation caused by their absence cannot be exaggerated. Rommel's personal experience in the years emphasized both the problems related to solid decision-making and the issues that face even the most experienced people under the condition which seems unsolvable for them.

The emotional voyage of Rommel's tragedy and subsequent rehabilitation seems to illuminate the fact that, through his absence, he took part in a potentially devastating and long-lasting event in the war period. The lack of his leadership, even if it was for a short time, was a huge force behind the German downfall. His finally coming back didn't heal any damage caused to both the strategic and the moral parts of warfare. The course of his incapacitation and recovery is the most touching fact that had to be paid for the human casualties of the military actions, and the willpower to lead from the forefront remained indomitable even when encountered with serious personal problems.

Rommel's Final Months and Tragic End

It is no surprise that the end of Erwin Rommel's career was characterized by the overwhelming of having lost faith in the Nazi regime and being simply heartbroken at the end of an era. As the war was increasingly gravitating against Germany and Rommel's reservations about Hitler's military and related policies went on over a year, his feeling of depression at the situation was even more dramatic. Moreover, he nearly claimed Hitler's life in the February 20 Plot, although being so indirectly, and therefore, it turned out to be almost fatal with the regime hunting him down.

The reason Rommel always bashed Hitler in the final months was because he disagreed with the talking head's insistence on not moving if the enemy did not attack and not allowing any local retreats even if necessary. Thus, Hitler's ill-conceived policies on many occasions, which were oblivious to the real gravity of the situation, only anchored the enemies and the worsening of Germany's army condition. No wonder Rommel was resolute in his view that poor leadership drove the nation to a debacle, as his knowledge of the battlefield and its operational aspects was second to none.

Nevertheless, it was in 1944, in the middle Roman's mood was forbidding at the time, he, told the truth. Plants on the war front were deteriorating at the same rapid pace, which meant Rommel was pessimistic about the prognosis. He was dispirited in not being able to conquer on the battlefield but he also didn't believe that a war would stop a goal or dream. Rommel's evergreen soldier reaction set him up as a very dogged defender of the nation. His convictions and his valoratism don't allow him to become a Nazi. In fact, his belief in the whole project of Hitler's dream was overthrown and he was more of an adversary to the Nazi way of life than anything else.

This was the strong disillusionment over the inability of Germans to end the war that led to Rommel's participation in the July 20 plot. This was a conspiracy carried out by the top German officers and civilians who wanted to remove Hitler from power and then do negotiations so that a peace treaty can be made with the Allies which could save the Germans from their complete destruction. Despite the fact that Rommel did not have any direct role in the planning or execution of the whole assassination attempt, he was one of the conspirators, and echo of his expressed desire for reforms made him a target after the failure of the plot.

July 20 Plot was the grim outbreak of the cruel reprisals. The Gestapo, had been given the job to fish out and severely punish those who were involved in the plot, started a massive search. Rommel's name came up in the interrogations of other plotters, and his previous bad words about Hitler and the regime were the final nails in the coffin. For Hitler, the discovery of Rommel's active participation, even if at the edge, was a huge letdown. Rommel was one of the two most admired and at the same time most activist military persons in Germany, and being disaffected by him the atmosphere became very unfavorable to the regime.

If sincere threats were allowed to trigger a Gestapo investigation and Hitler's ultimatums were to announce distrust, Rommel was faced with an impossible choice. Hitler gave him a simple ultimatum: either undergo a public trial, receive disgrace and die execution, or die quietly, protecting himself and his family from persecution. This was a well-thought-out strategy by Hitler to spare not only a possible martyr in 1942, but also Rommel as a war hero. The institution was supposed to maintain an honorable front of bravery and loyalty even as it dealt with those it considered traitors.

On October 14, 1944, Rommel poisoned himself. The story given was that he died as a result of getting injured in Normandy, which gave the regime the opportunity to hold a state funeral with all the military honours to be used. This was a sort of a shade which was done to keep the secret of his death while making him a national hero. The lying version of Rommel's death was the best example of the regime using propaganda methods to/ in order to further its own interests.

Rommel's death is like a tragedy of the great visionary and good commander who used to be admired. His final days brought the problem of his personal values and thus proved the way he has been handling tyranny issues. The way Rommel acted was tragic and it made Germany, as a nation, experience a larger tragedy during this war. Even great military leaders were in trouble within the Nazi leadership that they were once so loyal to.

The burial service of Rommel was a sobriquet of irony. Although the main intention was Rommel to be seen as the real hero, the truth of his despair and involuntary killing remain as the biggest defect of the idea. The façade of unity and power was more important in the eyes of the regime than it was to acknowledge the massive dissent and conflict that figures such as Rommel held. The last scene of falsification was just a short expression of falsehood and cruelty that plotted the Nazi movement.

Nevertheless, Rommel's fame is not dependent on the propaganda and the poor situation of his life and death. He is still one of the best military strategists in the 20th century, who is known for his original plans and leadership in Africa and Europe. His determination to oppose Hitler, even at the expense of his own life, sets up the conflict and loyalty together with moral conviction in the chaos of the war as the main subject for the whole story. Most importantly, Rommel's hectic life and death help in the realization of the personal costs of resisting oppression and the profound moral paradoxes by those who choose to overthrow the repressive political leaders.

To look back at Rommel's last months, one can not help but be amazed at the depth of his sense of betrayal and the moral dilemma that characterized his last days. His transformation from a victorious begetter to a disillusioned co-conspirator symbolizes the corrosive effect of strategic and ideological disagreements because of his profession. His ascendency as the "Desert Fox" is parallel to significant barriers and the tragic finale of his life, however, he is a model to those embracing heroic traits, like loyalty, duty, and moral conviction, in the most challenging moments. He tells us about the special human ability to bear and retain integrity in the face of insurmountable adversities and regrets that he could not have done otherwise.

Rommel's Last Campaigns and Enduring Legacy

The last chapter in Erwin Rommel's career that lasts for a few final days is the one that exposes the closure of his military life and the end of his life. Here he has some small victories, against the Atlantic Wall Ciego units of the department, also manufacturing the artillery required for D-Day. It seems, at first, that as long as he physically survives, he can manage to balance these two dangers with some small victories through negotiations but this protection ends when traumatic injury causes him to be sectioned. These last four battles, including his attempts to strengthen the Atlantic Wall and his daring the invasion of Normandy to his injury and the near end of his life were the, unfortunately, tempestuous end of a wonderful and bright career. Rommel did accomplish his Rwanda mission, born to be the "Desert Fox" master tactician remains, in fact, a hero, and was also very committed in time of war and also took part in other battles, which ultimately led to his death.

The Pacific Front also saw rampant pilfering in 1943 which result led to repair work and patrol boat activity that cost=7 days the Headquarters of the command in Saipan whereas it took 3 men 5 minutes to steal 100 dollars; the recaptured money; 50 dollars late were returned to headquaters.

Nevertheless, his attempts were in vain as June 6, 1944 the Allies launched a major amphibious assault on Normandy marking the turning of the tide. The D-Day landings, part of Operation Overlord, involved Allied troops storming the beaches of Normandy, overpowering the German defenses. Rommel, then back in his muddled zone, had seen the risk of the invasion in Normandy, but ultimately, he was misguided by being in Germany, visiting his family. His absence at the most important time of the invasions resulted in the loss of leadership which hindered the Germans. Rommel developed strategies and called for counter-attacks but the Mexican soldiers had the numbers and they were supported by better air and sea support which made it impractical to repel the invasion. The success of the Allies at Normandy was a disaster for the German forces in Western Europe.

Rommel had an attack in the car on the 17th of July, 1944 when he was the most severely wounded he had ever been. It was a group of fighters from the Allied side who attacked Robel. They caused him multiple skull fractures and severe facial injuries, and he was out of action for some time. Although the fall was hard and slow, he recovered and in Herrlingen, he stayed at his house for weeks. In that time, Rommel learned firsthand about the worsening condition of the war at all points of the compass. His injury was the reason for the loss of his physical and positional capabilities in the war and that was the worst move of the war for his military that was hoping for an alien.

The last months of Rommel can be referred to as the time of the period in which the disillusionment was his characteristic. His annoyance with the war strategic, and as a result, dramatical change in the progress of Germany did not come. This disillusionment peaked in July when the assassination attempt of Hitler through a conspiratorial method was materialized. This attempt was done by officials and civilians in collaboration to remove Hitler from power and conclude a peace pact with the Allies. He only had a minor role in the plan that was aborted by the Bessemer steel plants, but his term in jail was a result of his connection with the circles. After failing the plot, Rommel was the guilty party and was given the beginning of the Gestapo inquiry and received an ultimatum from Hitler. He had to choose between a public process and a shamed family to be spared and a quiet suicide for himself and his offspring.

Rommel lied about his death, saying he died from a wound in Normandy on October 14, 1944 when he ingested poison (cyanide). The Nazi government ordered him a funeral (state) to avoid the truth getting out that he committed suicide thus letting him be a brave one who was loyal to his nation. His death was a mark of the end of a career that had at one time been a model of excellence and creativity. His last months were tragic because the personal and ethical troubles he had with his service under such brutal leadership were so severe.

Rommel's story is very moving and makes us think about the price that people have to pay for war and the moral dilemmas that those involved in conflicts have to face. Still, even though the end of his life was tragic, Rommel will forevear be remembered as the "Desert Fox" and his legacy will never die out. His expertise in the field, his leadership, and the moral courage he showed in his last days of life are still being talked about and researched. Rommel's experiences are centered on the clash of duty, loyalty, and moral conviction, portraying the deeper personal and ethical problems which military leaders experience during war.

Rommel in his final campaigns and last days, which are the chapters of the book, is explored in detail from his preparations at Atlantic Wall, to his role during the Normandy invasion, to his being shot and coming back to life, and finally to the heartbreaking events that led to his suicide. These events were not only the end of Rommel's career but also they reflect the entire war and the internal tensions within German military authority. Rommel's unshakable mindset tempered with his inventive strategies in warfare is a forever demonstration of the complicatedness of command and the resilience of the human spirit.

By looking at Rommel's last few months, we can perceive the enormous personal and professional pressures that he endured. His battle to survive the political infighting and not lose his principles also presents the whole issue of the basic conflict between duty and morality. Rommel's story gives full play to the narrative of exceptional moral courage, sacrifices, and the profound effect of ethical leadership even during the most complicated times. He has left a similar legacy to the one that his exploits sparked in history, namely, of a hero who is both a man of integrity and a man of resistance in times of great crisis.

Chapter 9

Personal and Family Life

Rommel's Marriage and Family Life

Erwin Rommel's marriage and family life were among the key factors in his life that he used for balance at the time when he was affected by different things such as his military career. Rommel married Lucie Maria Mollin in 1916, during the World War I. Through his marriage with this woman, he got stability which made him grounded, and this was intensified by their loyalty and deep love for each other. Their relationship was very close from the beginning on the basis of respect and affection, and both exercised the love towards each other. She, known as the "Rock of Rommel," sustained his career's success along with the domestic life, running the house and making the surroundings look normal even when everything went chaos.

Their linking to each other was established on a mutual respectful admiration as Erwin outlined. Lucie was not only a very faithful wife, but she was also a date and counselor. The household was run by her with Professor Baxter and she was a good member of the army without having to consult the family. Lucie was not just a home-keeper, she was also very attached to her house, providing her husband with the necessary mental support and even assurance in times when he was down, especially in his career.

Copies of letters and photographs evidence the way their joint journey survived the trials and separations that life in the military is full of. Rommel to Lucie's letters showed the strength of their relationship. It was those letters that showed to many his inner thoughts, despair, and expect being a proud soldier he is. Rommel, in letters, manifested his thankfulness to Lucie for always keep up and not affected by his absence. Her correspondence reflects a mutual relationship of trust, love, and the joint belief that they are devoted to each other and their family.

The Rommels had their only child named Manfred in 1928. As the father, Rommel was a father who was full of love and affection for his son, even with his busy military schedule he was always willing to become involved in Manfred's development. He used his letters to express his unconditional love and worry for his son, proposing solutions as well as giving moral support. Rommel was especially interested in infusing Manfred's mind with the virtues of discipline, honor, and resilience, which guarantees that he grew up with a clear moral spectrum.

The family never lacked unity. Lucie and Manfred were the pillars of Rommel's stability throughout the years. Besides being a mother, Lucie's support also extends to her as the one who takes care of creating a safe environment for Manfred to grow. The way in which she endured the challenges of viability during wartime was with, if not, greater dedication and resolve as her role as a wife in Rommel's life was no different. A sense of mutual help and unity has been the characteristic trait of the Rommel family arising from the strong bonds that virtually held them together.

It was very clear that Rommel's love for his family was paramount in his thoughts and his decisions. He put his family's welfare above all even during the most troublesome times of his career. Some of the correspondence to Manfred served as a mirror that reflected his ideas of education, character, and the value of perseverance. Thus, his ambition to be the anchor and positive role model in his son's life was clearly discernable despite the fact that they often dwelt in two different places.

It can be concluded that the family was the only peaceful harbor for the Rommel. The comfort and confidence from his family provided the courage to deal with the professional challenges. Lucie played the vital role in retaining that stability; she was just indispensable in the housekeeping and in providing the necessary moral support, and this, in turn, empowered Rommel's ability to fulfill his military duties in an effective manner.

Rommel's family union greatly enhanced his perspective on things, and that was a significant factor in the formation of a different method of running things. His self-control, bravery, and being capable to overcome the difficulties of his personal life were the attributes he displayed in his relationship with the public. Rommel's love for his comrades and his capability to be the reason for devotion and respect in them had various backgrounds but all of them were based on the values he had while growing up with his family. The sense of truthfulness and commitment which he was showing as a husband and father was parallel to the respect he dominated in the field of military.

The Rommel family's years passed during the Second World War were full of both: pride and misery. One of the biggest drawbacks of Rommel's occupation was the fact that long periods of time separated him and his family, and due to the risks of his occupation, Lucie was constantly stressed. Burrowing the bonds of unity, the Rommel family remained undisturbed in the light of these various challenges, which were made possible through the efforts and love of each family member. The participation of Lucie and Manfred was neither solely passive nor was it restricted to Rommel's professional life only. They were actually the core based on which he stood and moved through his life.

The commended psychic development of Erwin Rommel's family-both marriage and personal life-is not limited to military victories only. The bound of his relations with Lucie and Manfred has been more solid illustrating that family is the support and the key to the loved one when it comes to mental peace and balance. This points out the human angle of a person who is primarily recognized for his strategic genius and military prowess. A person's capability to adapt to the requirements of his job and at the same time to fulfill the commitment given to the family is the proof of his character and quality.

Reflecting on Rommel's marriage and family life offers a more coherent picture of the man behind the military legend. It shows a man that loved his wife and kids and held the to be honours of honor, discipline, and endurance in both his daily and professional life. The sturdy and unified family support given by Lucie and Manfred, were the top two factors that enabled Rommel's return to Germany and the difficulties of his long career. The most obvious result of their relationship is that they have never stopped the power of family relation and thereby the vital role of the playful environment at home which ensures the strength of even the busiest of lives.

A Strategic Mind at Leisure: Rommel's Personal Interests and Hobbies

Erwin Rommel, hailed for his remarkable military tactics, enjoyed a wide range of pastimes and hobbies that were a restful escape from his strenuous job. These were not just his entertaining activities but the main components of his strategic mind and fulfilling overall life. Rommel's personal life had a strong bond with nature, as he was a passionate reader of military history and strategy, leading him to a liking of mechanics and engineering that he had loved since he was a child.

Rommel has a special liking for nature and outdoor activities. Nature seemed to be the very inspiration behind Rommel's passion for it, among other things, he used to hike and look around the beautiful environments that lay around his house. His intimacy with nature provided him with the essential relief that he needed and in contrast, it acted as the antidote to the pressures that his military duties put on him. Rommel's quiet walks with wildlife repaired him and helped him to recollect his mind and receive fresh insight, which was indispensable his strategic planning and decision-making.

Rommel's natural adventures contain the need for him to find clarity and focus, not just the pleasure nature brings. The studies of hiking and the difficulty to pass the woody paths wittingly reminded him of the strategic thinking. This independent time allowed him to abandon the immediate encroachments of his job and take part in freestyle meditation; he could remember what happened and make some thoughts. The body movements and mental relaxation he had brought him by nature would be positive attributes of his strength and mental attaining his full potential on the battlefield.

Rommel, who was a zealous reader, showed a militaristic atmosphere when he said about the military history and battle strategies he adored the most. He had to deal with serious subjects like the presentations of the works of the military theorists and the historical figures. His insatiable desire for knowledge was not just passive reading but was an active endeavor to always better his grasp of war and leadership. The books that Rommel kept at home were old ones such as the "On War" by Carl von Clausewitz as well as Helmuth von Moltke the Elder, of which he overly studied.

It can be deduced from the above that Rommel was not only a dictator of knowledge in relation to the military, but he actually went beyond it. He actively promulgated his comprehension of internal and external, foreign and domestic politics by the shifting theories and tactics employed in his own command. This unique mix of methodical study and empirical technique was manifested in his groundbreaking methods on the battlefield. Romans must adopt new solutions quickly in war and they do not have to trust conventional transmissions as well because they profit from master minds writing and understanding military history in a profound way. The cognitive endeavors were the basis for the understanding which gave him the tools necessary to strategic flexibility, thus providing him with a wide and well-stocked reservoir of knowledge for use in his military campaigns.

Furthermore, Rommel who was utter in his collaboration with military literature did not only acquire the knowledge-theoretical version of what he was reading but he actually ensured to use the knowledge he got in his strategies and tactics. This stems of the concept of theory and practicality that was seen in two of his new ways of handling different situations on the battlefield. Rommel's ability to respond and experiment with new situation as well as his lots of use of unusual tactics were essentially the cause and effect of the seemingly endless reading and in-depth perspective it

[@#88e5d6 content] had in the world of war history. His intellect even assisted him in getting a change of the angle and get the source of the crucial information for his military campaigns through his reading pursuits.

Rommel's fervor for mechanics and engineering was indeed a large portion of his leisure time. Back from hardly toddling age, he showed enormous interest in the functioning of the things, and this zeal matured into a lifelong study. It should be noted that it was a purely academic experience; Rommel went past the normal by giving practical application to the knowledge he acquired. He was engaged in various studies where he spent countless hours taking a piece that wasn't working and trying to get it to work again. Also, he had practical engineering skills developed.

This mechanical draw became his life, workwise, quickly he said that when it comes to his innovations, they are tactical ones. The usage of tanks and mechanized units by Rommel was his pioneering idea. Actually, his interest in engineering was the one that made him directly operate mechanical units and tanks in his military operations. What could make him the best military strategist was his intimate knowledge of the functioning and possibilities of these machines. In this way, he could make them useful during the war. His new methods and lightning war, for example, were based on the mechanical and artillery power that a mechanized unit had. He could move easily and quickly, which helped him nothing but defeat the enemy with his new style of attacking. Rommel's engineer-like point of view allowed him to see that defeat is nothing but a challenge, but for others it is a complete block. This was the opinion of him as a theologian of tactics.

The personal side of the committed soldier was also the base of his battlefield strategies it was one of his secrets of success which was his entire life. His ultimate love was for nature, intellectual activities, and engineering, and they were not activities without which he was whole. Quite the contrary, they were the most important component in his personality which determined the development of his thinking and actions. The synergy of personal interests with professional duties provided him with the edge of becoming not only a better leader but also a catalyst for the team.

Rommel excelled in his professional as well as personal life indicating the depth of his character. Even if the work was difficult, he still managed to find peace and fun in things outside. One of the things that Rommel had clear was that leisure and intellectual development along aside one's duty in life are necessary for a soldier to be successful and healthy.

Inserting a peek into Rommel's personal life and hobbies can let us into the man who was known to the world as a fearless and victorious soldier. This man had a mind of both discipline and curiosity, so Rommel was a perfectionist, and still, he was learning and discovering every time he was amidst nature, in the books he read or the new technologies he practiced. In his days a man lived a life of high professional dedication and multiple hobbies that resulted in a lifetime of success that he can be proud of.

In the awareness of Rommel's personal pleasures, individuals accomplish development of his never-give-up spirit, creative thinking, and strategic mind. His whole story is a reminder for every life about the importance of the right choices in life, both personally and professionally. Rommel's contribution to the world is not just a military gifted person but also a person who had a wonderful life, a life occupied with a ceaseless search for knowledge, a close tie to nature, and a constantly enduring interest in the mechanics of living things and battles.

In His Own Words: The Personal and Military Writings of Erwin Rommel

We more clearly know very closely with the innermost thoughts, emotions, and multi-dimension of his personality through the letters and personal writings of Erwin Rommel. The written works of the artist who communicated with the members of his family from a personal perspective and, at the same time, wrote various tunnel documents as part of his military work comprise the image of the leader as the warm person he was when outside the military circles. They depict him as a man completely devoted to his family, who values the culture of honor and duty, and for whom the quest for knowledge and perfection is an enduring mission.

The most impressively most of the letters YN his wife Lucie show this. For, they too, were letters of a loving man who at the same time was the extraordinary husband and father, the mythic hero, which to general opinion, he was not. The Rock of Rommel, as cogently called her, was his solace the confidant and his emotional anchor. These dialogues were the means by which Lucie would listen and contemplate on such issues as to Rommel's service to the land, strategic both, and his personal feelings. To Lucie, who is his favorite, Rommel is always giving expressions of his sheer gratitude for her continuous assistance and excellence in managing the household in his extended absences. These letters also bring to light the generals big concerns and hideings, and thus, give us a tiny peephole at a mans weaknesses who otherwise appears to be invincible.

Consequently, Rommel's letters to Lucie show his analytical and strategic thinking on the ongoing war and his points of view. He would comment on the difficulties he faced, his conclusions based on the battle areas, and his dreams on a bright tomorrow. These documents are not just official records of the past but also intimate talks that visualize Rommels strong and tender feelings for his wife and reliance on her calmness. Hence, they not only present the human part of a leader but also reveal Rommel as a person fundamentally influenced by his personal and ethical combat during the war.

The epistles that Rommel wrote to his son Manfred are just as significant. Dad was giving the considered explanation and some important pieces of advice, he focused on the qualities of honor, duty, and courage. Rommel's priority was to bring up Manfred as a responsible and principled individual. These notes were often practical guidance and self-reflections on what he considered of value like morality, steadiness, and observation of the right direction.

Rommel, in his letters to Manfred, was the avenue of sharing his own experiences and teaching Manfred the same lessons he learned during his time in the army, thus helping his son identify his morals. He told Manfred to be curious and have the guts to ask questions in the unpleasant times and urged him to maintain the highest standards of behavior. These letters written to Manfred show Rommel's solid commitment to his family and his intention to teach and encourage his son while being far away. They embody the father's devoted care and the responsibility that was not restricted only to the battlefield. He in.

This is not connected to these personal letters only, though. Rommel's own military writings bring out both an accurate description of his experiences and tactical insights. His "Infantry Attacks" (Infanterie greift an) is generally considered as a military strategy classic. Infanterie greift an, first published in 1937, was a book full of every detail of the author from the time of World War I giving us clear directions about his tactical thinking and approach to combat. 'Infantry Attacks' was well received for its practical tips and accurate descriptions of stressful battle scenes which testify to Rommel's analytic capability and his ability to get knowledge from errors.

"Infantry Attacks" is the best example of how Rommel gave priority to initiative, flexibility, and aggressive action. These were his leadership style principles in the Second World War. Furthermore, the book is a reflection of the belief of Rommel in the need for the soldiers to change and adapt to the dynamics of the battlefield, as well as the lessons he acquired from his battles. His skill in aggregating experience into general tactics is a proof of his yearn to read and to impart his knowledge of military strategy and leadership to a broader audience.

Rommel's military writing is characterized by its easily understandable contents and strong focus on practical issues. His main goal was to provide insights to future leaders based on such experiences and emphasize their applicability in different combat scenarios. His writings, in different words, give insights into past fighting and they become guidelines; for instance, they stress the significance of adaptability, courageous, and the use of diverse military means to win the battle.

The personal and military writings of Erwin Rommel reveal the doublet of a husband and a soldier who values his family just as much as he does his military duties. His letters bring out the emotional side and individual trouble of a person who is often best known but through his endeavors on the battlefield. They underscore his unwavering focus on his child and wife, his thoughts on the ethical dimensions of warfare, and his dedication to the qualities of honor and duty.

Other sources note Rommel's military career. For instance, there are some brief remarks in the book about his daring tactical maneuvers and, due to which, gains to trade. The writings express not only his voracious appetite for the subject but also his goal to teach lessons he has learned from his life to the armed forces leaders of the future. As a result, one gets the chance to admire the sage Erwin Rommel, the one that laughed and cried, the faced his inner demons. It extensively demonstrates the link, both personal and professional, that he had within the different aspects of his life.

It is the understanding of Rommel's personal interests and writings that leads one to the causes of his strength, originality, and ingenuity. His life is a universal flick and he capitalized on every bright scenario he can reach along his voyage. There, he makes a strong claim for integrating not only work responsibilities but also individual aspirations that help in enriching and improving one another. However, not such a kind of narrative only comes up with military performance, but basically find in his entire life the virgin the knowledge dealings, a slew of intimate thoughts to the family, and a deep that s amidst life and war are related.

The Heart Behind the Warrior: Rommel's Personal and Family Life

This chapter deals with Rommel's private life, especially the fact of his life, which abstracts him from the military procedures, and reveals him as a man who was always stronger than difficulties. Aside from what was made public, her relationship with Lucie Maria Mollin and their child Manfred showed a different aspect of Rommel. It is a side that will never shy away from his family and personal interest but one that is attached to them inseparably. On his part, these bonds furnished him with the emotional assistance and calm he needed to face the challenges of his occupation.

Rommel's connection with Mollin on Lucie became his life support. They got married in 1916, the period of turmoil of World War I when they were extremely loving and mutual in their respect for each other. Sometimes, Lucie was described as the "Rommel's Rock," regardless of severe and frequent moves, was steadfast in his stand by her side. She was an excellent homemaker who ran their house efficiently and smoothly so that Rommel had a safe and loving place to come back to after the war. Their partnership was not of one soldier and one spouse but of two people who let each other into their lives completely, with Lucie providing not only emotional stability but also practical help.

Their boy, Manfred, born in 1928, was the main focus of Rommel's private life. He was a beautiful father, well-kept and interested in the child even though he was very busy due to his many military activities. His letters mostly communicated to him his deep love and the comprehension he had though those mostly stood as advice and direction. Rommel primarily embedded virtues like hard work, integrity, and stout-heartedness into the boy, with the view of making him a responsible and law-abiding citizen. They formed a close-knit family, and the attachments between Rommel, Lucie, and Manfred become the lasting source of his mental wellbeing.

Rommel, except for his family, enjoyed lots of mind-entertaining hobbies and activities outside his job. Nature became the center of his interest and one of the most prominent activities was his excursions. The outdoors was something Rommel was deeply attached to, and he often spent his time there hiking and enjoying the beauty of nature around his home. The fact the father was intimate with nature was a double-shot of rest and rejuvenation; it made him less stressed because nature itself is the opposite of the pressures of military responsibilities. Rommel's ability to be in the quiet and vivid place of nature was very helpful to him in chasing his aim of coming to his senses and stepping back so as not to lose his decision power.

Time spent tackling his intellectual interests was also an essential area of Rommel's life. To the reader with broad interests in the military history and strategy of the world, the constant study of influential figures in the military history and the critiques of the famous military theorists was his part and portion. He was not superficially acquainted with such matters; he was studying them with a vigorous desire to be always the best teacher, strategist, and commander. This article addresses an instance of Lamar's mech topics: his invention of the camera and the automatic machine gun designed for use in the army of the government, which the more recent and more advanced models will incorporate. Moreover Rommel's interest in mechanics and engineering which he had been attached to since he was a kid was a key factor in both his personal and military life. He was a felicitous pupil of mechanical things at an early age, and this enthusiasm for technology grew into a lifelong dream. He had his personal way of working with the mechanical projects, and then he applied this in his professional career by using them in the production of tanks and mechs. It's the blending of engineering principles and the ability to become hands-on on each machine that waded the most new era of tactics for him especially through his engagement in Blitzkrieg tactics. His watchword was visualizing of several options where others saw insurmountable stumbling blocks, which was a striking feature of his strategic way of thinking.

Rommel's letters and personal writings are his clear self-revelation while doing what is more. His chat with Lucie and Manfred is the talk of a man who is infinitely wedded to his family in good times and in bad times of career - his words are so deep and touching. Frequently, he cites his experiences and ideas, and his deepest feelings. A more closely-knit study of Rommel is given to us. His vulnerability, his profound family love, and his invariable information form the nucleus of the letters.

Besides his individual correspondence, Rommel's military textbooks such as his book "Infantry Attacks" (Infanterie greift an) also present a verbose picture of his military missions and tactical knowledge of World War I. This path-breaking book on military tactics brought out the real image of Rommel as an analytical thinker and as someone who could get to the core of his experiences. His writing is a clear way to show his self-education and the way he tries to improve the military skills and lead. The book "Infantry Attacks" got the fame for its down-to-brass-tacks counsel and the exhaustion of war-related incidents like Rommel's way of dealing with the situation.

This part talks about Rommel's personal family interactions and the chapter gives the whole picture of a man who was undoubtedly living the craziest era of history and yet classically anchored his love to the family and his deep passions he was engaged in. This feature points out the humane features of Rommel, which, in turn, complete his image of being remembered not only as a military leader but also as a husband, father, and a person with a highly developed inner life. His marriage to Lucie and their joint company with Manfred are the sweetest example of a person who is very close to his family, thus his personal relationships are the base of his final success.

Rommel's personal interests and hobbies disclose his not only keen intelligence but also a passion for scanner. This man had been interested in not only relaxation but also strategic thinking and innovative ways all of which along with the destruction of his military endeavors brought to his life. The correspondence and the personal writing of the person give us an intimate insight into his mental life, which includes his thoughts, his values, and also personal struggles.

Through the examination of the personal life of Rommel and his family, the chapter emboldens the interpretation of his legacy, which brings up the idea of a man who was a perfect mix of being a military officer and at the same time was committed to his family and also enjoyed different personal hobbies. The significance of the human factors that make up Rommel's being is emphasized, bringing to the forefront a new direction of thought for one among history's most well-known military performers.

Chapter 10

Legacy and Historical Impact

Master of Maneuver: Assessing Rommel's Military Leadership

Erwin Rommel's commander who stood as a display. He is one of the most notable leaders of the 20th century who could be called a model commander. His approach to leadership had such a hands-on style, he led from the front and through his own personal example inspired his troops. Rommel on the other hand, was a true master of blitzkrieg, which was the particular method he used to perform these maneuvers, especially in North Africa, where it was the most difficult, and for a commander not previously famous for this battle, had to figure everything out. This superior treatment is what certified him to be one of the most skilled tank warfare practitioners in the world, a title he wore with pride. Counterparts to this valiant display of initiative were his emphasis on flexibility and aggression. They were the crowning achievements of his leadership style, without which he couldn't have been so successful.

Rommel is one of the leaders who really showed the best way to go, his belief in the leadership from the front was really significant to his leadership style. Rommel was a great part of every operation while other leaders would always be the ones to force their troops to the front lines. During this time he was on the battlefield and could use first-hand information to make his decisions that were based on the reality of combat. All at the same time, his being with the soldierson the battlefield augmented the high spirit and togetherness of the unit. The soldiers would find more confidence with a leader who shares the dangers and sufferings with them.

Besides his readiness to put himself in danger, he had already proven that he was someone worth trusting.

One of Rommel was quite able at... was the fact that he could execute quick and decisive moves. The Afrika Korps were the organelle of the African sojourn where he served. The hostile desert conditions were supplanted by his comprehension of mobile warfare to take advantage of the environment. He was so skillful at attacking with speed and mobility that he could enter the enemy's rear to take them by surprise. He mainly, nonetheless, turned the situation around by his military cunning in the Battle of Gazala and the Siege of Tobruk.

Rommel's insistence on flexibility and flow of initiative was the core of his command philosophy. He suggested that the commanding officers must be given the opportunity to exercise their judgment and act in accordance with the circumstances, without being tied up to an inflexible plan. The control allowed his subordinates to function with some degree of freedom, and that was indispensable in the flexible and fast-moving nature of mobile warfare. Rommel directed his officers to snatch the chance when it emerged and, by this way, he produced an atmosphere of proactive and adaptive thinking among his troops. This elasticity made his troops to deal with the changing conditions of battle in a good way, to make out of them the occasions for winning.

Introduction of aggression could hardly be omitted from speaking of Rommel's leading. He was remarkable for his determination to dominate the game by hassle the adversary. He most of the time used military aggression as a means of solving a problem. The one prediction he encountered at that point of time was very difficult to predict. Successful offensives are the result of his system of aggression, and even his minority defeated the enemy many times. This way of injuring caused an extreme disorientation to his opponents along with establishing a sense of collective effort and purpose among his troops.

Rommel's logistics genius was not confined to his tactical mastery but also encompassed his logistic planning. He realized the pivotal role of supply lines in the extensive desert and thus he put forward uncommon actions to maintain a steady flow of essentials. Defensewise his commanding the troops for prolonged battleships was fought aside from the logistical problems thus became an undeniable proof of the strategic and experienced planning he had. It is Rommel's god foresight in the logistic aspect that made the troops follow the orders properly and swiftly enough to maintain leadership.

Rommel did not limit his leadership to his victory on the battlefield but he influenced the military strategy and tactics even after decades of World War II. Most of the modern military doctrines are characterized by the concepts of flexibility, initiative, and rapid maneuver which Rommel always used in his operations. The essay "Infantry Attacks" is the main source of information for the military professionals all over the world because it gives an insight into his tactics and strategies. Rommel's legacy as a military thinker and strategist persists as the evidence of the immutable value of his contributions to war art.

His personal qualities such as the ability to motivate his troops, leadership and mobile warfare mastery, and his ability to think differently were the other aspects that were magnified by his professional merit. His fearlessness, decision-making, and inexorableness were the keynotes of his leaders. These characteristics gave him the control to provide a solution to problems in tension, prop up the animal of his forces, and even cause successes in some places where the odds were near to impossible. Rommel displayed a combination of both strategic intelligence and personal gallantry thus he became the prime example of leadership which is still significant now.

Erwin Rommel, to a large extent, was a competent commander who had cumulated his strategic brilliance and innovative tactics that stood out of the other commanders in the 20th century. The reason for his success was his active involvement, commitment to the fastest and most decisive maneuvers, and the implementation of the value of initiative, flexibility, and aggression. As a result, he became a prominent military leader in the new era of military aviation. The soldier represents the significance of the solidarity of man, which could be achieved both on the battlefield as well as in the area of military history in general.

Pioneering Tactics: Rommel's Enduring Influence on Modern Warfare

Modern warfare has been drastically and lastingly changed by Erwin Rommel. His unconventional methods and strategic principles not only form the basis of research and application by military planners all over the world but also serve as the stepping stone for many other innovations. Rommel was the first to apply the Blitzkrieg tactics, the use of quick strikes, synchronized movements, and the involvement of infantry, tanks, and airplanes, to armored warfare, as well as to defense-in-depth concepts. Leading the way, his ideas the fast and unexpected use of resources among others, are the main reason why they are glorifying use in the army, and have gone further into training and operational planning in the army.

Lightning war is the core of Rommel's tactical legacy. This was a strategy where Rommel would order his troops to hit the enemy line very fast directing most of the fire-up front and afterward, the enemy troops would not be able to gather themselves together for a common defense. Rommel executes his Lightning War method in the most visible way when he takes campaigns to France and North Africa. The protection and police actions were achieved quickly with the Allies' help and made the soldiers feel stunned. Rommel's proficiency in operating an assault of this kind with the masterful use of mobility and flexibility became a powerful aspect in the modern battlefield.

The use of Blitzkrieg tactics by Rommel not only provided speed and surprise components in conducting his campaign but also showed an advanced combination of arms operations. By combining the three forces--the infantry, armor, and air support, Rommel created a single fighting force able to counter the variety of battlefield issues. Moreover, this combination became the catalyst for achieving the highest efficient level in combined arms operations as the army could give maximum damage by the means of joint operation. The excellent cooperation in between these forces under Rommel's guidance let quick redeployment regarding the regime of the battlefield go in favor of the cutting down of enemy weaknesses efficiently.

One way that Rommel left a lasting impact on the military was through his emphasis on rapid movement to perform maneuvers that will help the military operate more effectively, and thereby advised the military to prioritize movement over those of potential adversaries (Mitcham 6). The security of the natural buffer of the mountains that stood between the two warring sides leads to his strategic decision; he moves into France and arranges his soldiers to take on a decision. Rommel was always focused on to save time in movement, so his high operational tempo was because of speed.

Variability is a challenge that all military leaders are to face in decision-making, on the battlefield among other areas. However, tactical flexibility which is a quick change to a tactic also became one of Rommel's strengths; consequently, he used it as his major force multiplier. It explained the practice of the military operations to the newcomers. He was confident that his troop movements would terrify and confuse the Allies resulting in major troop movements, thus disrupting and disorganizing their formations.

Rommel equally attributing to somewhat thankless work in all of these operational fields would utilize infiltrated resourced to compensate for Russian lapses and quality second-rate human resources. Establishment of Geological Shoreline Observation Network for the purpose of cloud optical thickness from a well shaped ridge on the shoreline of River Nile to Alexandria. Again in 19th, none-zone homogeneous conditions were configured along the Rs/SI axis to the coast of the Siberian region, which are longitudes.

Rommel's way of war-making which is his mark on warfare of the 21st century goes beyond his tactical innovations. His texts, specifically "Infantry Attacks," go into detail about his (the author of the selected text) experiences and tactical insights that are not only exclusive but also they are very useful for military professionals. The principles stated in his work are also what the military education and training programs are based on this, then those training programs are essential for military operations and military strategy, thereby training programs and tactical operations effectively providing the military with such tools and capabilities by expression of examples and exercises. Rommel's insistence on taking risks, being able to adjust, and not hesitating about the decision to be made are the main thoughts of the strategy courses, like the one that he proposed on battlefield, which proves his great influence on the perception and practice of warfare.

Rommel's policy has actually an impact on the scale of military tactics in the modern world by including several of these new doctrines and operations. The traits of quickness, good delivery, and joint ventures which are essential he proposed are the ones that were bought and polished by the armed forces after it won its acceptance and establishment due to designing by the armed forces worldwide. The modern military operations, such as the USA's rapid deployment forces extension and the conducting of joint operations that involve air, land, and sea capabilities operating in conjunction are the modern operations that are influenced by this. The Israeli Defense Forces' won implementation of Blitzkrieg-influenced tactics in the Six-Day War is an additional reason for the sharpness and the timelessness of Rommel's strategic insights.

Rommel's style of command and control forming by his will to adapt to new requirements enriched also with his security of decision changed the whole attitude of military leadership. His initiative of commanding from the front in-the-spot decision-making based on instances supported military authorities, which had to modify the methods of leading the army. Modern military leaders are ordered to be observable and in position, signaling the troops their readiness to be with them in risk and danger situations. This leadership style builds trust and interaction inside military units, thereby boosting their fighting capability among other skills.

All in all, Erwin Rommel was an enormously influential figure in contemporary warfare. His introduction of Blitzkrieg tactics, his exclusive promotion of the speed and surprise elements and his original link-up of arms of different types in combat set new standards in military strategy. Rommel's thoughts on frugal utilization of scarce resources and his hands-on works in military education have become the very foundation of the military principles and operational planning of armed forces across the world. As a master tactician and strategic thinker, Rommel's impact is obvious, stressing the everlasting relevance of his precepts in the modern warfare situation, where every new step requires new adaptation.

Rommel: The Controversies Behind the Legend

Although Erwin Rommel is a well-known personality for his military skills, his journey is not a conflict-free one. The intricacies of his connection with the Nazi regime, his part in the July 20 Plot aimed at killing Hitler, and the questions of morality and ethics he had to deal with during the war raise a shadow on his reputation. Even though Rommel was not a member of the Nazi Party, his professional relations with Hitler and the fact that he was the face of the Wehrmacht gave birth to the impassionate argument about his political views and complicity with the regime. This piece is going to discuss the contested parts of Rommel's service, which are his diverse experiences and the moral questions that he had to navigate.

Rommel's connection to the Nazi regime is the most emphatic discussion point in his career. Although he never joined the Nazi Party, he became popular under the leadership of Hitler, who provided him with all possibilities and the necessary resources. Hitler adored Rommel for his military skills and therefore put him in the position of a good model officer in the Nazi propaganda. Because of the close professional bond, some even did not exclude the view that Rommel was also a Nazi for his political views. Though there is no hard proof that Rommel actively supported the Nazi ideology, his blind acceptance of the Führer and obedience to the regime's commands open a way to tackle other already important issues.

Rommel's interaction with Hitler had both positive and negative shades. Primarily, Hitler was a big Rommel fan who considered him as a talented young officer who would play a major role in strengthening the German armed forces. The victories of Rommel in the initial years of World War II, especially in France and the WAfrica-north area, made him a mighty man of the army. Still, the tides of war turned unfavorably for Germany and the bond between Hitler and Rommel became tensed. The main reason for this was that Hitler's thinking revolved around the idea of offensive warfare while Rommel was more practical, results-based, and less lover of theory. Thus, they would often be together in logic derivation but apart on the choice of the right strategy.

Rommel's attempt to assassinate Hitler during the July 20 Plot was the controversial point of his career. The German defeat was near, and a group of high-ranking German officers and civilians wanted to eliminate Hitler and sign a peace treaty with the Allies. Rommel's role in the conspiracy is still a matter of historical controversy. The fact is that at least he was the one who supported the idea that he had to be eliminated and he was a senior with the help of others. He wanted to let Germany live longer by doing so and therefore his involvement in a plot where the changes have been small and very discreet was mainly due to the circumstances he was in and the reason he would have to overcome. He did it because he was not happy with the dictatorial authority Hitler was carrying out and he advised that peace was the only way Germany would escape utter demolition. On his part, he was slowly pulled over to the side of a coup due to his desire for a new government and his fear of more deaths.

Rommel was very careful about being part of the July 20 Plot, indicating that he was somewhat practical and had a good understanding of the risks involved. He was part of the planning or even the killing of the leader, but he was not actively involved in it. Any good leader knows that failure has terrible consequences. At best, the evidence of his involvement with the conspirators was not so obvious at once when the plot had failed. Hitler had one last maneuver against Rommel; that was to either let him be judged before the public and then executed or to let his family live by taking away his own life instead of giving Rommel his wish of his family being safe from any reprisal. He, on the other hand, took an overdose of cyanide on October 14, 1944, completing his decision to die this way rather than being tortured. He was declared dead on another front where he had earlier been injured, and the Nazi government arranged a state funeral, thus keeping the assumption alive that he was an honest and loyal person.

Rommel's career also raises controversial questions about his ethical decisions and actions during the war. His behavior toward the closed POWs was the so kind that in most cases one could only compare him to the far more brutal characters of other German commanders. In fact, very often Rommel would tell them how they should take the captured soldiers and not hurt them as well as follow the rules of war. Due to this he was very well respected by both friends and foes. Nevertheless the frame of his service in a military corps which supported the mass killings evil doings and many others makes the measure of his moral integrity more subtle. Rommel was not causing the great holocaust but nevertheless, his standing as a leader in the German army was invariably a part of the regime's actions.

The partisan stances of Rommel on the Jewish genocide raised another controversy. It can be proven that Rommel was not aware of the full extent of the Holocaust nor was he informed about its mass killings of Jews and other vulnerable ethnic groups. At the same time, he was not utterly ignorant of the genocides as well. He was exposed to certain information to which he did not react. One varying interpretation of his silence is to look at the situation from a military tactic view to another being that it was his own failure to take a stand against the atrocities that he had knowledge of. The regulative face of his silence in particular reigns as the key thread binding the debate that has been going on for many years.

In addressing the disputable aspects of Rommel's carrier, it is necessary to take into account the period in which he lived. Forces like approval with modern communication, thinking and norms were then in existence in his day. Also, the personal danger that he faced as a renegade was another contributing factor. The press in his lifetime put it like this: the fact that he targeted no civilians makes him an absolute hero. His saga is a reminder of the tough decisions and inevitable compromises often made under a tyrannical government or within a dictatorship.

Rommel his legacy is really the complex and multifaceted one. Yes, he was really right to celebrate his military genius and the new movement that focused not only on the theory but also practice, however, the other parts of his military career are forgotten. His adherence to the Nazi party, his participation in the assassination plots of the July Revolution, and his moral and ethical choices during the war all revealed a deeper, more complex and often conflicting character. Through the sides of his life and career, Rommel was a debatable character should people reflect on the issues he overcame because of his not giving up the life he is.

Rommel's Place in History: A Complex Legacy

Erwin Rommel was not only a military commander, but a historic figure as well. His military achievements and the historical setting of the Second World War era have made him the identified person. Fast and furious mobile warfare was the hall mark of Rommel's successful military career. He fought the French in the spring of 1940 and commanded some divisions in North Africa where he showed great skills in using mobile warfare, especially the Blitzkrieg tactics. He completely recast the form of war to an integrating style of the three fundamentals of warfare such as foot soldiers, guns and air power intertwiningly to make flexible and dynamic military organizations, the likes of which nobody had seen before. Rommel outstandingly his performances during the first two years of World War II in France and North Africa well showed his novel method of waging was treated more like a chess game keeping a sharp look out for the changing phases of such a battle. His on-the-spot creation of strategies surprised both even his own defense and its opponents, and the exclamation of his being the greatest of the war's commanders swept away any shadow of doubt about his origin.

One of the hallmarks of Rommel's career is his military genius. He is known to be the one who was behind the "Desert Fox" project in North Africa campaigns which he both masterminded and was physically present in the battles himself, as the head of a squadron of tanks. He made the surprise attack his own adaptation of the maneuver, thereby elongating the duration of the battle, thereby favoring his own side and upsetting the enemy one. Furthermore, Rommel's biographers have pointed to his strategic skill as showcased in his northern Morocco conquest as an example to follow. His wit enabled him to both create and exploit the course of battle to this end, whereby he was able to win several battles hustling the weak Germans in various corners of the globe. Victory in the whole war of all time was his, and was in fact made against only the former axis powers, without the participation of the nazi's, as it can be seen by the victors of the state of occupation of the north west corner of the Soviet Union, all of Falaise, Inn, and Ardennes, who are also plotting against the French upon the Nazi conquest of certain additional territories. The peaceful coexistence of the Allied and German blocs as well as of former axis powers is one of the primary goals of the victors. In such a context, there would surely raise certain disputes which must be discussed peacefully.

However, Rommel was not solely famous for his military talents. His name is closely associated as a high-ranking officer under the Nazis and his commitment to the German military made him a widow of controversies regarding his politics and the link between him and their regime. Though Rommel was actually not a member of the Nazi Party, he was quite inclined to follow the tendencies of Hitler that gave rise to his otherwise sudden development. His partnership with Hitler which involved only respect and need to implement the military strategy among them made the characterization of Rommel as a military leader without any political aspirations less straightforward. The moral question on his leadership of military forces under a regime that should be deemed unacceptable because of its despotism remained the cause of disagreement.

With his affiliation in the 20th of July Plot to undermine Hitler, Rommel's biography is getting more and more complicated. Though the exact nature of his role in the plot is still under discussion, it is clear that Rommel was at least sympathetic to the points of view of the conspirators. The very prudent way he got involved insinuates his gradual disenchantment with Hitler's dominance and his conviction that the only plausible option for Germany which would ensure its survival was getting out of the war before the total annihilation would take place. Rommel's affinity with the conspiracy plot leading to his later forced suicide calls attention to the moral and ethical dilemmas he faced as a senior military officer. This side of his historical character is used as the illustration of the internal struggles and hard choices that his last years were made up.

After the war, Rommel's reputation developed dynamically as various versions tried to decipher his deeds and personality. In Germany, he started out as the hero who bravely fought for his country while distancing from any Nazi ideas. One of the factors contributing to this narrative were the ones who tried to depict the image of the German army in a beautifiable way that would also eliminate the element of war criminals. The ways Rommel treated prisoners of war and his opposing certain policies were brought to the fore to support this differentiation.

Rommel is one character in the numerously pictured world of popular cultural and historical facts. Cinema, literature, and documentaries have been powerful tools for both the embellishment and denunciation of the myth of Rommel as the "Desert Fox." The 1951 film "The Desert Fox: The Story of Rommel" and the 1953 film "The Desert Rats" were veiled instruments in shaping the public's view of Rommel as a man who fought honorably and gallantly. During the war, these over-the-top images of the Desert Fox, as a master in warfare and an impeccable moral person, were far more beneficial to the Allied propaganda than reality.

Further historians have indeed been the basic method of criticizing and explaining Rommel's inheritance. Nevertheless, it is a wrong perception of the early historiography that has been focusing on his military accomplishments and his contradictions to specific Nazi orders. The recent scholarship has new historians of which have focused their point of view on the Rommel topic from the criticism side rather than from the point of rejoicing. The positions of the historians have taken into account Rommel not as an isolated character but as an element within the entire system, paying special attention to his involvement and the ethical values behind his service. This complex view emphasizes Rommel's tactical genius, while it takes account of his ambivalent ethical career that was full of contradictions.

The fact that he was loved in history is also the result of the myths and realities that surface his personae. The myth of the "Desert Fox" is a product of many forces such as the war propaganda of the time, the attempt to rehabilitate him in the postwar period and his recurrence in popular culture. Despite the fact, this myth has significantly contributed to Rommel's depiction as a tactical expert and his building a reputation as an honest warrior, it has belittled the more controversial aspects of his career. The actual evaluation of Rommel could be given a mixture of factual accuracy, which is the descriptions of his important influence on military strategies and the ethical problems that his involvement in the violent regime raised.

Actually, Rommel's location in history can be seen as the net of relationships that connect both his military deeds and the ethical issues he faced. His brilliant tactics in the field and military meme different in nature influenced the development of this area. Even though he was a perfect strategic example in the war period, the Nazi association and the fight against his thought compel the story to have contradictory ends. The person of Rommel is a true illustration of the ties of military leadership during the wars that can be as complex as in the case when strategic superiority would go hand in hand with moral dilemmas of different nature.

The heritage of Rommel has always been a subject for hot debates and reflections, thereby, laying emphasis on the full relevance of his life and career related to the understanding of historical developments as complicated as they are. Rommel who contributed the most to the military strategy and showed ethical behavior is the best example for the military leaders of today and for the historians as well. In contrast to him, whose legacy has been discussed for a long time, we can finally find the beauty of the complex personality of the man and the broader historical context he lived through and served.

Rommel's Complex Legacy: A Balanced Reflection

A chapter on Erwin Rommel's legacy and historical influence brings together all aspects of his military tactics, his connections to modern warfare, and the misunderstandings in his career. This chapter, by investigating the diversity of the Rommel's impact, attempts to offer a balanced and multilayered evaluation of his role in history, paying tribute to his extraordinary accomplishments and at the same time drawing attention to the moral ambiguities of his career. To this end, Rommel has been fortified by history and currently, he is a man being discussed whether accepted or not and the consideration of his total influence is indispensable in the debate.

Erwin Rommel's military strategy remains a defining characteristic. The usage of his smart approaches and his insights into the sphere of mobile warfare have changed the direction of many military doctrines. Rommel's first Blienschein-like tactics demonstrated the power of simultaneous high-speed assaults of coordinated, easily moved armored units, thus paving the way for the development of the heaviest of tanks re-enforced by well-armored vehicles. His ability to involve the infantry, armor, and air support in the formation of a flexible and competent defense force was influential and it led the modern militaries to follow similar patterns of activity. His approach to the military, especially in its relation to speed, surprise, and miserly expenditure of resources are traits of military strategy that are still pertinent, and they serve to confirm his everlasting reputation in this genre.

Nevertheless, Rommel's life has been a source of conflicts and struggles as well. His professional partnership with Hitler and the Nazis produce the nuance in the account of his life. Even if he didn't belong to the Nazi party, he was victorious because of the opportunities provided by Hitler, and was frequently shown as a model officer in Nazi propaganda. This situation has become the ground for the controversies still going on around the political views of Rommel and his cooperation with the regime. The problems posed by Hitler came to light through the man's will to work with him, and his obedience to the regime's rules raise some very essential ethical issues that must be considered.

One of the most controversial things about Rommel's career is his participation in the July 20 Plot to kill Hitler. When the German army was on the verge of defeat, Rommel became more and more disappointed with the way Hitler was leading the country, and he slowly took part in the conspiracy. Rommel, who was barely involved, was aware that by reducing the destruction a war could stop Germany from dying soon. The plot failing along with the illegal step being taken by Rommel as a way of his coercion to suicide are the great examples of the moral and ethical dilemmas a man from his position has to go through. This episode introduces another viewpoint to his life, the interpersonal conflicts and the professional challenges were the defining aspects of his last century and were mostly conflicting to each other.

Another point to be considered in what concerns the ethics of Rommel during the times of war was also his treatment of the POW. He was generally humane to prisoners of war, and among those that were not only on the level of other officers, but also more humane as compared to the inhumane rules of the German commanders. Rommel frequently himself told the soldiers to follow the rules of war which earned respect from both his comrade soldiers and his enemies. Nevertheless, the decision to not discuss the bigger war crimes in which the Nazis were involved may compromise the pattern of his morality. There will hardly be any concrete evidence that Rommel was directly involved in or open to these offenses, but his standing as a Wehrmacht officer inevitably pointed to his collusion with the regime. The main points of the ongoing argument about the general attitude towards him contain this sort of ethical uncertainty.

Rommel's legacy changed in different ways in the post-war era. At first, in Germany, he was the character that was redeemed. This redemption of the military was done with his death and the soldiers were all instrumental in bringing Germany back from the depths brought on by the World War II. This line was at its most vulnerable when it became necessary to restore and highlight the image of the armed forces and to split up the real fighters from the Nazi criminals. Rommel's sensitivity toward the captives and his opposition to certain Nazi policies came out of this. This picture was utilized for reforming the reputation of Rommel as a knightly and nice person, whose popular image was moreover endorsed by the euvre of literature, art, and film.

Through portraying Rommel as the "Desert Fox," movies, books, and documentaries have been a crucial factor in forming the Rommel's image. Among works like the 1951 movie ""The Desert Fox: The Story of Rommel"" and the 1953 "The Desert Rats," the romanticized view of Rommel as a brilliant tactician and a man of principle have been the main contributions. Despite the images, which are almost always exaggerated, that have been created thus, Rommel's status as one of the most famous military heroes of the Second World War remains unshaken. Nonetheless, historians adopt a more sober view, assessing not just Rommel's actions in the context of the Nazi regime but also examining his complicity and the ethical implications of his service.

What makes Rommel's legacy so intricate is the myths and the facts existing to this very day concerning him. The "Desert Fox" myth is the result of a combination of military propaganda, post-war reconfiguration measures, and pop culture. This story brings to light Rommel's military brilliance and his standing as a brave fighter and in doing so, it usually displaces the disagreements developed over the course of his career. The true legacy of Tierphalis is, on the one hand, profound military developments and, on the other hand, moral questions raised during his tenure under the rule of a ruthless government.

The place of Rommel in the future is, in the end, a matter of the very complex relationship between his military achievement and the moral and ethical dilemmas patience he has. There are no disputes about his brilliant tactical maneuvers and battlefield achievements that were profound and far-reaching. On the other hand, the question of his association with the Nazis and the controversies revolving around his political beliefs and actions bring a touch of complication to his legacy. The tale of Rommel is a living symbol of the confusion of leadership during war times, wherein strategic prowess is juxtaposed with moral questioning.

Based on the many different sides of Rommel's heritage, this chapter will deepen our understanding of him as a military commander and as a personality who has been established as a source of argument and meditation. Frank Rommel's ideas about military strategy as well as his moral and ethical behavior are relevant for today's military leaders and historians too. The evidence of his existence puts the spotlight on looking at historical characters in the context in which they lived, giving both the positive and negative dimensions for a better and deeper look at their input into history.

Conclusion

The Life and Legacy of Erwin Rommel: A Comprehensive Overview

With a description of Erwin Rommels childhood and the impact of his family, the book opens. The Thoroughness of Education His Family Gave Him Discipling was discussed, and even the name of his origin, that is, Heidenheim, Germany, where it was born, was then described. Rommel was given the blend of the educational and the characteristic of the conscious use of different types of educational systems and of social awareness at the same time a military academy. Father Erwin Rommel Sr., a teacher and the last of the headmaster, played an important part in shaping Rommel to become a well-educated adult and to develop a systematic way of problem-solving. Due to this nurturing educational environment, Rommel was assigned to being nicely comparing to his practical awareness and his methodical style as these were all necessary to his life in the army. Rommel's mother was born as Hellene-Benz and married a father who was specializing in the military needing for a little nobility in the military Arched German interior used it unto if book measures more than 75025 pixels wide with the outermost corner of the entire entity at its center and the unit is square a grid having a spacing of 12.5 micrometers becomes such that the graphics containing the largest texts and images have an approximate width of 125 micrometers. His parents were the foundation of his great reach for further outcomes.

Rommel's career in the military is traced in detail paying attention to his joining the German Army and then his first assignments. In 1910, at the age of 18, Rommel entered the 124th Infantry Regiment as a leader cadet. His fresh military style, sealing with the dedication and excellence, his performance was not doubted for long and so he was a shooting star. In 1915, Rommel 8217s reviving exceptional skill at the front lines especially at the Battle of Caporetto, displayed a tool kit of tactics and unmitigated bravery, thus he managed to get several prizes including the prestigious Pour le Mérite.

The narrative becomes Rommel's years between the two World Wars, focusing on his professional growth and his contribution to military literature. He was still part of the Reichswehr, the organizations that followed the Imperial German Army, and aside from the training he was implicated in the process of formulating strategies. Rommel wrote "Infantry Attacks" is as the book is set, a book that explicitly indicates fully him and hisius being thought of in his own wayl he offerded his own views on thbright war that he had first entered.debuted such a remarkable work during such a crucial time. Not just that, Romme's book also served as a blueprint for German military doctrine in the run-up to World War II. Rommel's progress in the Wehrmacht was remarkable, but what stood out isthe the story of his incy thebility to adapt to the rapidly changing military conditions.

Rommel's early role in World War II is presented as a means to demonstrate his military skill and command style. His account of his time in France, and the 7th Panzer Division which he commanded, known as the "Ghost Division," were the most significant examples of his mastery of Blitzkrieg tactics. His quick maneuvers, such as using high-speed armoured vehicles and successfully combining all three forces, allowed his soldiers to win battles very fast with full triumph. His ability to keep the French campaign under control as he inspired the troops, and outperformed the challenges, encouraged him to become to be one of the most successful of the commanders in the Nazi regime.

The Bolshevik being noted can also be seen since the main attention is on the North African campaign. The book "The Use of Blitzkrieg in the Libyan Desert" translates the whole story to the main event that was leading the troops to achieve certain significant goals and using this to prove the superiority of their army. Appointed by Hitler as the leader of the Afrika Korps in early 1941, Rommel was acute in his strategies. The main battles that took place then are cases of Tobruk and Gazala show that taking the advantages of the mobility and the firepower of his armoured units was the way that he established his victories. His greatness in the North Africa campaign, on the other hand, raise his nick-name "Desert Fox" and at the same time stress his capacity to reach large operational objectives in the face of the difficulties he had who were largely logistic in nature and the harsh desert weather.

The book draws attention also to the more controversial sides of Rommel's life, such as his connections to the Nazi regime and his participation in the assassination of Hitler through a bomb at Wolfsschanze. Rommel, although never joining the Nazis, found a way to collaborate with Hitler and his high-ranking position in the Wehrmacht. This, in turn, has caused much dispute over his personal opinions and the extent of cooperation with the government and what really happened. Rommel's role in the July 20 Plot was a deliberate decision on his part, one that was motivated by his growing disillusionment with Hitler's decision-making skills and his eagerness to see an end to the war. His inclusion in the plot, even though not a big part, made his life filled with many torment and so he ended this in October 1944 when he committed suicide by forced means.

The book also discusses the ethical and moral issues Rommel encountered while the war was happening, especially concerning how he dealt with the prisoners and his point of view regarding the atrocities that were committed by the Nazis. His respectful actions towards the prisoners of war and his efforts to observe the rules of warfare led to Rommel being esteemed not only by his allies but also by his enemies. Nevertheless, taking into account the fact that the overall environment of his service in Wehrmacht and his silence regarding the cruelties committed by the Nazi regime, it challenges which side of the ethical issues he falls on.

This summary finally examines the post-war legacy of Rommel, centering on his character's portrayal in the media and the ongoing debates about his life. Initially, after the war, Rommel was depicted as a valiant hero who had the courage to fight for his country along with staying ambivalent concerning Nazi ideology. This narrative was mainly guided by the necessity for Germany to restore the military's image and separate professional soldiers from Nazi criminals. To enforce this kind of perspective, actual situations of Rommel's respecting human rights and defying a number of Nazi beliefs are stressed.

Rommel is arguably one of the few characters, recognized in popular culture, who is either vilified or romanticized, from filmmakers such as the German filmmaker Fritz Lang to the antagonistic portrayal in Hollywood movies of him which greatly varies. Films, books, and documentaries have played a significant role in shaping the public perception of Rommel, both in his military superiority and the ethical pitfalls of his career. Historians usually judge Rommel by focusing on the context of the Nazi regime and analyze the complicity of Rommel with the regime and ethical dimensions of his service.

Through an examination of the ambiguous nature of Rommel's heritage, the book makes an effort to understand an objective and thorough evaluation of the Rommel era in history. The writings of Rommel on military strategy as well as his moral and ethical decisions offer today's youngsters as well as the leaders of the army a set of them. The narrative of his life is a clear elucidation of the twisted path to leadership during wartime that brings together the issues of strategic wisdom and moral dilemmas. The survival story of Erwin Rommel remains as a searing invitation to the battleground of his life and career for those of us who are really into unraveling the complexities of history.

Reflections on Rommel: Legacy of a Military Genius

When we look back at Erwin Rommel's career and the impact he made, we are given the opportunity to understand that his strategies in military are still of great importance. Rommel's original maneuvers, mainly his pioneering of the so-called Blitzkrieg and joint arms operations, are among the factors that have left a clear visible imprint on modern warfare. His tactical priority of speed, surprise, and flexibility remains to be a vital contributor to some military doctrines and training that happen around the world making it know from the outset that he has an impact in modern conflicts also.

Rommel's method to Blitzkrieg, he did fast, intense, focused attacks with the idea of outnumbering the opponent, was the thing that really changed the nature of armored warfare. This pointer's favorable outcome in his excursions in France and North Africa had shown the value of rapid and well-organized offenses. By combining infantry, tanks, and air support into the focused and flexible fighting units, Rommel established a new criterion for combined arms operations. The modern approach to the army stick to these cardinal points as well, which in other words means that Rommel changed the way wars are fought even today.

Also, under the attributes of uniqueness, Rommel's style of leadership can be another issue by which this matter can be thought. His engagement and ability to stimulate his soldiers through personal acts made him an excellent leader. Rommel himself was one of those brave leaders who took cover from enemy fire with his soldiers and had the same living conditions as the ordinary soldiers during campaigns. His unique visibility and involvement on the battlefield developed a strong sense of loyalty and respect for his men. Rommel's skill of organizing high morale and unit solidarity, even when faced with insurmountable conditions, was a real manifestation of his amazing leadership traits.

Rommel's stress on the decision-making skill and the capability of adapting also made Rolfe very successful. He was of the opinion that leaders should be the ones to take decisions according to the present situation rather than following preset plans strictly. This idea facilitated his troops to be able to respond rapidly and effectively to the various conditions of battle. Rommel's guiding principles of leadership, which fostered such qualities as flexibility, speed, and personal example, have given rise to the present-day discussions on which styles of leadership are most needed, thus affirming the lasting relevance of his own classic leadership concepts.

The discussion grouping together the ethical and moral issues of Rommel's career is given an in-depth look at as well. Negotiating the terms of his professional relationship with Hitler and the Nazi government was a stumbling block. Although Rommel was never an affiliation with the Nazi Party, his relationship with the party and his high profile in the Wehrmacht made the historians continuously search for the answers about his political beliefs and his level of connection with the regime. The ethical dimension of Rommel's career was a significant burden, especially pertaining to the loss of life of prisoners and his position on the brutalities committed by the Nazis.

So what concept of humane treatment of prisoners of war did Rommel bring forward to distinguish himself from many of the other contestants for greatness? He never failed to instruct his men about the conventions of warfare, and to this end, he not only got respect from his friends but also from the enemies. This nature of his behavior reflects an endeavor to maintain the standards of morality in the middle of a brute war. On the other hand, Rommel's inertness in the cover-up of the over-all the more crimes done by the Nazi regime adds a touch of complexity to the issue of his moral standing. Although there is no proof that Rommel has explicitly been included in the war crimes, his fortuitous position in the German military hierarchy indisputably tied him with the conducts of the regime.

The prudently fleeting deed of Rommel in the July 20 Plot to kill Hitler further shows the ethical and moral contradictions he found himself in. Disenfranchised with Hitler's leadership as well as the future of the war, Rommel that castration Hitler was a must for the country to stand up. Although his promotion of the conduct of the plot (on the side) marked his actively expressing opposition to the regime. The failing of the plot in tandem with the subsequent blame and Rommel's subsequent suicide brought to light the sadness of his career and the encompassing entangled personal and professional differences he had to cope with.

Moreover, the articles also represent Rommel as he is depicted in the general public and in historiography. Several narratives have been aired over the years, portraying him in different ways, from the idealized picture of the "Desert Fox" to the more dissecting literary works. Through films, literature, and documentaries the great mind was paradoxically created and the historical personality was disclosed. Complimentary and yet critical representation was made of the character often times, these are only the former though, which strongly emphasizes the heroics of the soldier. Estranged from fiction, experts attempt to make out the whole story and its intricate play of lose ends, endorsing or not dissatisfying facts and statements.

Perceptions of the personality of Rommel show the complexity of these and his life. The idolated depiction of the "Desert Fox" accentuates his tactical genius and his reputation as an honorable fighter that frequently eclipses the disputable parts of his military career. The real legacy of Rommel comprises notable military contributions as well as the perceived ethical issues he created in association with the Nazi government.

The chapter ends with a brief review of Rommel's experiences from which military leaders and historians can derive modern military lessons. It highlights the importance of situating individuals within their epoch, realizing the achievements and shortcomings of each. A defining term of Rommel's heritage is a showcase of the intricacy of leadership in the situation of armed conflict, and thus, presents valuable insights on the conflicts and ethical issues actors in the military services have to deal with.

Rommel's account underscores the interspace of strategic genius and ethical uncertainty, maintaining that a holistic and meditated approach is the best way to comprehend historic personalities. His impact on military strategies along with the moral and ethical decisions he took continue to lead to heated discussions and thoughtful conclusions, bringing into focus the fact that his life and career remain significant today. By tackling various facets of Rommel's legacy, this section adds more depth to our realization of him as a military leader and as a character whose life and career are still relevant in the broader scheme of history.

Appendix A

Timeline of Major Events

Early Life and Career

- 1891, November 15: Erwin Rommel is born in Heidenheim, Germany.
- 1910: Rommel joins the German Army as an officer cadet in the 124th Infantry Regiment.
- 1912: Rommel receives his commission as a lieutenant.

World War I

- 1914-1918: Rommel serves with distinction during World War I.
- 1917: Rommel plays a pivotal role in the Battle of Caporetto, showcasing his tactical ingenuity.
- 1918: Rommel is awarded the prestigious Pour le Mérite for his bravery and leadership during World War I.

Interwar Period

- 1920s: Rommel continues to serve in the Reichswehr, focusing on training and professional development.
- 1937: Rommel publishes "Infantry Attacks," detailing his experiences and tactical insights from World War I.

Early World War II

- 1939, September: Germany invades Poland, marking the beginning of World War II. Rommel commands Hitler's personal escort brigade during the campaign.
- 1940, May-June: Rommel commands the 7th Panzer Division during the Battle of France, earning the nickname "Ghost Division" for his rapid and decisive maneuvers.

North African Campaign

- 1941, February: Rommel is appointed to lead the Afrika Korps and is sent to North Africa.
- 1941, April: Rommel begins the Siege of Tobruk.
- 1942, May-June: Rommel achieves significant victories during the Battle of Gazala.
- 1942, July: The First Battle of El Alamein halts Rommel's advance into Egypt.
- 1942, October-November: The Second Battle of El Alamein marks a decisive defeat for Rommel, forcing a retreat.

Later World War II and Final Campaigns

- 1943, March: Rommel is reassigned to oversee the defense of the Atlantic Wall in France.
- 1944, June 6: The Allies launch the D-Day invasion of Normandy. Rommel returns to his command in an attempt to repel the invasion.
- 1944, July 17: Rommel is severely wounded when his vehicle is strafed by an Allied aircraft in Normandy.
- 1944, October 14: Rommel is forced to commit suicide after being implicated in the July 20 Plot to assassinate Hitler.

Legacy and Historical Impact

- Post-1945: Rommel's legacy is shaped by both admiration for his military tactics and controversy over his association with the Nazi regime.
- 1951: The film "The Desert Fox: The Story of Rommel" is released, contributing to the romanticized image of Rommel.
- Ongoing: Rommel's contributions to military strategy continue to be studied and debated, reflecting the complex nature of his legacy.

Appendix B

Key Military Decorations and Awards

Erwin Rommel, renowned for his military prowess and leadership, received numerous decorations and awards throughout his career. These honors reflect his bravery, tactical ingenuity, and significant contributions to the German military efforts during World War I and World War II.

World War I

- Iron Cross, Second Class (1914):

  - Awarded for bravery and leadership early in his military career during World War I.

- Iron Cross, First Class (1915):

  - Awarded for distinguished military service and acts of valor on the battlefield.

- Knight's Cross of the Royal House Order of Hohenzollern (1917):**

  - Awarded for exceptional leadership and bravery during the Battle of Caporetto.

- Pour le Mérite (1917):

  - Germany's highest military honor during World War I, awarded for extraordinary leadership and tactical success, particularly noted during the Battle of Caporetto.

Interwar Period

- Weimar Republic Decorations:

  - Rommel received several medals and decorations for his continuous service and contributions to the Reichswehr and later the Wehrmacht during the interwar period.

World War II

- Clasp to the Iron Cross, Second Class (1939):

  - Awarded for his leadership during the invasion of Poland.

- Clasp to the Iron Cross, First Class (1940):

  - Awarded for distinguished service and leadership during the Battle of France.

- Knight's Cross of the Iron Cross (1940):

  - Awarded for his exemplary leadership and tactical success in the Battle of France.

- Oak Leaves to the Knight's Cross (1941):

  - Awarded for his outstanding leadership and successes in the North African campaign, particularly during the early stages of Operation Sonnenblume.

- Swords to the Knight's Cross with Oak Leaves (1942):

  - Awarded for continued excellence and leadership during the North African campaign, including the Siege of Tobruk and the Battle of Gazala.

- Diamonds to the Knight's Cross with Oak Leaves and Swords (1943):

  - One of the highest honors in the Wehrmacht, awarded for his exceptional leadership and tactical brilliance throughout his North African campaigns.

- Afrika Cuff Title:

  - Awarded for service in the North African theater of operations.

Posthumous Recognition

- Rommel has been commemorated in various forms posthumously, including military studies, popular culture, and public memory, reflecting the enduring complexity and significance of his legacy.

These decorations and awards highlight Rommel's significant contributions to military strategy and his exceptional capabilities as a military leader. They serve as a testament to his impact on both World War I and World War II, acknowledging his tactical brilliance and leadership qualities.

Appendix C

Selected Bibliography

This selected bibliography provides an overview of key sources and literature used in the research and writing of this book on Erwin Rommel. These works include primary sources, such as Rommel's own writings and letters, as well as secondary sources, including biographies, military histories, and scholarly analyses. This collection of references offers a comprehensive foundation for understanding Rommel's life, military career, and legacy.

Primary Sources

- **Rommel, Erwin**. *Infantry Attacks (Infanterie greift an)*. Translated by G. E. Kidde. Athena Press, 1944.

  - Rommel's detailed account of his experiences and tactical insights from World War I, providing firsthand perspectives on his military strategies.

- **Rommel, Erwin**. *The Rommel Papers*. Edited by B. H. Liddell Hart. Harcourt, Brace, 1953.

  - A compilation of Rommel's personal letters, diary entries, and other writings, offering valuable insights into his thoughts, strategies, and personal life.

Biographies

- **Fraser, David**. *Knight's Cross: A Life of Field Marshal Erwin Rommel*. HarperCollins, 1994.

- A comprehensive biography that explores Rommel's military career, personal life, and legacy, providing a balanced assessment of his achievements and controversies.

- **Lewin, Ronald**. *Rommel as Military Commander*. Batsford, 1968.

A detailed analysis of Rommel's military strategies and leadership qualities, with a focus on his campaigns in North Africa and Europe.

- **Young, Desmond**. *Rommel: The Desert Fox*. Harper & Brothers, 1950.

- One of the earliest biographies of Rommel, written by a British officer who fought against him. This book contributes to the romanticized image of Rommel as the "Desert Fox."

Military Histories

- Barnett, Correlli. *The Desert Generals*. Indiana University Press, 1960.

- An examination of the key military leaders in the North African campaign, including Rommel, with a focus on their strategies and battles.

- Mitcham, Samuel W. Jr. *Rommel's Desert War: The Life and Death of the Afrika Korps**. Stein and Day, 1982.

- A detailed account of Rommel's campaigns in North Africa, analyzing his tactics and the challenges he faced.

- Neumann, Robert G. *The German Generals Talk*. William Morrow and Company, 1948.

- Insights from German generals who served with and under Rommel, providing perspectives on his leadership and strategies.

Scholarly Analyses

- Messenger, Charles. *The Art of Blitzkrieg**. Sterling Publishing Co., Inc., 1991.

  - A scholarly analysis of the Blitzkrieg tactics used by Rommel and other German commanders during World War II.

- Showalter, Dennis E. *Patton and Rommel: Men of War in the Twentieth Century*. Berkley Caliber, 2005.

  - A comparative study of two of the most famous military leaders of World War II, exploring their strategies, leadership styles, and legacies.

Popular Culture

- Chamberlain, Peter, and Chris Ellis. *The Desert War: The North Africa Campaign 1940-1943**. Ballantine Books, 1969.

  - A popular history of the North African campaign, including Rommel's role and contributions.

- Hunt, Sir David. *A Don at War*. William Blackwood & Sons, 1966.

  - Personal reminiscences of a British officer who served in North Africa, providing an opponent's view of Rommel's tactics and leadership.

Additional Sources

- Correlli, Barnett. *Hitler's Generals*. Grove Weidenfeld, 1989.

  - An anthology of essays on the leading generals of the Nazi military machine, including a critical analysis of Rommel's career.

- Goerlitz, Walter. *The German General Staff: Its History and Structure 1657-1945*. Reynal & Hitchcock, 1953.

- A comprehensive history of the German General Staff, offering context for Rommel's role within the broader military hierarchy.

This selected bibliography provides a robust foundation for understanding the multifaceted life and legacy of Erwin Rommel, offering readers diverse perspectives from both primary and secondary sources.